# Crowmarsh
A history of Crowmarsh Gifford,
Newnham Murren, Mongewell and North Stoke

Berenice and David Pedgley

Published 1990
by Crowmarsh History Group
35 Thamesmead, Crowmarsh, Oxon OX10 8EY

Typeset in Prestige Pica 10 using an Amstrad PCW 9512.

Printed in England by Parchment (Oxford) Ltd.

Copyright:
text and diagrams, Berenice and David Pedgley
drawings, Joan and Will Wilder.

All rights reserved. No part of this publication may be reproduced or transmitted in any form or by any means, electronic or mechanical, including photocopying, recording or any information storage and retrieval system, without prior permission in writing from the publisher.

ISBN 0 9516305 0 4

|    | Preface                  | 4   |
|----|--------------------------|-----|
| 1  | Settlements              | 5   |
| 2  | The Land                 | 22  |
| 3  | Farmers                  | 27  |
| 4  | Houses                   | 50  |
| 5  | Roads                    | 60  |
| 6  | The Church               | 65  |
| 7  | School                   | 79  |
| 8  | Craftsmen and Shopkeepers| 87  |
| 9  | Services                 | 99  |
| 10 | Sick and Poor            | 104 |
| 11 | Recreation               | 116 |
| 12 | Law and Order            | 126 |
| 13 | War and Misfortune       | 132 |
|    | References               | 144 |
|    | Subject Index            | 152 |
|    | Name Index               | 159 |

# Preface

In this book, we have tried to show how Crowmarsh has changed over the centuries to become what it is today, with emphasis on people and how they lived. We have relied on records, not hearsay. The records are mostly written, but the landscape also has something to tell us, both natural and man-made. We use the records not only to give an account of Crowmarsh history but also to show something of how that history is revealed.

The book is not laid out chronologically. Instead, we have chosen to illustrate various activities in the lives of all Crowmarsh folk: work, travel, religion, education and so on. Many records have been consulted but not all have been used in the book, which would become unwieldy and run the risk of being little more than a list of facts. Our selection tries to present a broad look at community life and its changes, steering a middle course between formal and anecdotal.

We have thought it useful to include references to our more unusual sources. They will enable readers to look more closely at particular events, and they allow us to justify statements we make. Evenso, we are aware that some statements may need changing as new records come to light or as known records are reassessed. We have not made reference to the common sources such as parish registers, censuses, wills and directories.

We acknowledge with thanks the help given us by record offices, libraries and individuals named in the reference list. We are grateful, too, for the contributions from other members of the Crowmarsh History Group: to David Beasley, for permission to use some of the photographs from his large collection; to Joan and Will Wilder for their drawings; and to Richard Lay for access to his local knowledge and for continual encouragement.

We also acknowledge the financial support towards printing costs given by Crowmarsh Parish Council, the Greening Lamborn Trust and the Wallingford Bridge Estate Charity.

Berenice and David Pedgley               Crowmarsh 1990

# 1. Settlements

'Crowmarsh' was a name given by the Saxons to an area of wet land bordering the Thames opposite Wallingford and presumably noted for its crows. Today, 'Crowmarsh' is the name of a civil parish, formed in 1932 under the Local Government Act 1929, only partly overlapping the Saxon land and containing the four ancient settlements of Crowmarsh, Newnham, Mongewell and North Stoke [1]. All four settlements presumably existed in Saxon times, judged by their names [2]. Crowmarsh can be translated literally, and Newnham means 'new village'. Mongewell is 'the spring of the Mundingas' - followers of Munda, a Saxon chief whose name appears in other places, such as Mongeham, Mundford and Mundham. Stoke means 'farm', or simply 'place'.

The earliest inhabitants, from the Old Stone Age, were hunter-gatherers, not farmers. They settled near the Thames because the valley was largely forested [3]. Although their tools have been found, as at Lonesome and Blenheim, there is no direct evidence of settlements in Crowmarsh [4]. With the onset of the last Ice Age these folk left and it was not until about 3,000 BC that New Stone Age farmers appeared. They grew corn and stored the grain in pits [5]. By starting to fell the forest they began the lengthy process of changing the landscape. Their flint arrowheads and tools (axe, scraper and polisher) have been found [6].

6                    Settlements

About a thousand years later the Bronze Age beaker folk arrived, so called from the habit of burying the dead with characteristic pottery under low mounds [5]. Following centuries of ploughing, the remains of these mounds can sometimes be seen in crop marks - green or parched areas in growing crops where the soil is deeper or shallower, respectively. In the field south of Cook Lane, North Stoke, a complex of circular and rectangular enclosures has been revealed, along with the burial of a child with a beaker [7].

Beaker folk settlements, and probably also those from the New Stone Age, would have been chosen with an eye to the availability of clean water. A perennial source has been the line of springs near where the bottom of the chalk rocks comes to the surface. Between Crowmarsh and Goring, this line lies close to the east bank of the Thames. At North Stoke and

Crop marks in growing corn, showing where there was a Bronze Age settlement at North Stoke, south of Cook Lane.                    (Ashmolean Museum, Oxford.)

Mongewell the springs are strong enough to drive water mills, but elsewhere they are weak and intermittent and, except after wet weather, give rise to little more than trickles draining to the Thames.

Around the fourth century BC, Celtic tribes began to appear, bringing their system of growing crops in small fields. Tribal or regional boundaries were set

Terracotta beaker, about nine inches tall, found at North Stoke in 1954 with the skeleton of a child from the Early Bronze Age (about 2000 BC).

(Ashmolean Museum, Oxford.)

up in the form of banks and ditches such as Grim's Ditch, which runs in a straight line for over three miles between Nuffield and the Thames at Mongewell. The purpose of Grim's Ditch is not known for certain but it most likely represented the boundary between two settlement patterns: on one side the light soils cleared first for cultivation and sheep-rearing; on the other side the later forest clearings whose farmers were concerned with pigs and cattle [8]. A ditch, originally 8-10 feet wide, was dug and material thrown up to the north to make a bank; a gap was left for Icknield Way. When the A4074 was widened at Ice House Hill in 1973-4 a length of Grim's Ditch was excavated and fragments of Iron Age pottery were found, though this does not conclusively date it. It certainly represented a massive amount of manpower. 'Grim' was another name for Woden, one of the Norse gods, and the name came to be associated with such a huge structure of unknown or presumed supernatural origin.

By the time the Romans came, in the first century AD, much of the valley forest had been cleared and farms on good arable land were scattered between the riverside swamps. Pieces of their pottery and tiles have been found in fields south of Crowmarsh Street, and a coin (a centionalis of Decentius) when a copse was being cleared on Grim's Ditch above Woodhouse Farm [9]. The Saxons, who arrived from the fifth century, took over the older settlements, giving them new names and adding others. Perhaps the 'new village' of Newnham was founded at this time.

In medieval times the kingdom was divided into a mosaic of estates, called manors by the Normans, owned by the king but held by a hierarchy of tenants in a feudal system. Those in the higher ranks held manors by fees such as knight service; those lower down the system held them by base services such as rents or farm work. The manor was essentially a unit of land, with both lord and tenants bound by manorial customs, upheld in courts that met once or twice a year to appoint manorial officers, decide agricultural practices, and try minor offenders. Sometimes the lord lived in the manor house, but often he let it to a gentleman or farmer. The tenants would be in cottages often grouped in a village. In more modern times, as land was often sold off, the lord's rights could become little more than formalities. In this respect, the histories of the four manors show interesting differences.

Except for Crowmarsh, which seems to have been carved out of a corner of the large royal manor of Benson, the estates supporting the settlements formed parallel strips from the Thames to the Chilterns, straddling the Icknield Way (see maps: inside front cover and p. 61). This alignment may have been guided by ancient tracks along which timber had for long been hauled down from the hills to the settlements. Whatever their origin, the strip estates provided a variety of land usage - meadow, arable, pasture and woodland - as well as a fishery in the Thames.

Manorial administration created many records but almost none is known from Crowmarsh. However, the records of central government, particularly from about 1200, although referring mostly to the higher ranks in the feudal hierarchy, do give us glimpses of medieval life in Crowmarsh, as well as illustrating the complexities of manorial holdings.

Following the Norman conquest, king William gave Saxon estates to his followers, some getting many estates scattered across the kingdom. Crowmarsh was divided into two: one part went to Battle Abbey (later known as Crowmarsh Battle, but being in Benson, it is not included in this history); the other went to Walter Giffard, Earl of Buckingham [10], who received 107 estates according to Domesday Book, prepared in 1086. Walter Giffard was standard bearer to William in Normandy, though he was too old to fight at Hastings. When his son, another Walter, died in 1102, the manor passed to his son, yet another Walter, then still a boy. After his death in 1164, it returned to the king because Walter had no heir. Subsequently, the manor came into the hands of William Marshall, who in 1189 had married Walter's distant cousin Isabel of Clare (in Suffolk) and thereby became earl of Pembroke. He died in 1219, but his son, also William, is recorded in the Fine Rolls for 1228 as appearing personally in the king's court to counter the claim of Wallingford burgesses that his men held an unlawful market in Crowmarsh. After William died in 1231 his estates passed successively through his four brothers, and when the last of them died in 1245, Crowmarsh manor passed to his niece's husband, William of Valence, a half brother of Henry III, made Earl of Pembroke in 1259, and who is recorded as holding the manor in the Close Rolls of 1249, the Feudal Aids (1285) and an inquisition of 1287 [11].

We can get some idea of the structure of Crowmarsh society around this time. An 'extent' of 1264 (in effect, an evaluation of the manor) shows there was an unspecified number of free tenants paying a rent of 74s 4d with 2lb of pepper, and cottars paying 29s 6d [12]. Cottars had to work the lord's land as a condition of their tenancy. By 1287, another extent lists 45 free tenants, paying 116s 5½d twice yearly (and the 2lb of pepper) but no cottars, so perhaps they had become free in the meantime [13]. Each tenant presumably represents a household, which can be taken to average four or five people, so the population then was about 200, more than twice the number three centuries later (see page 16). Perhaps this reflects the terrible loss of life due to the Black Death in 1348 (see page 106).

When William's son Aylmer of Valence died childless in 1323 the manor presumably passed back to the king and then to William's nephew Laurence Hastings, who became Earl of Pembroke in 1339. This earl is named in 1356 in the Black Prince's Register as having the manor of Crowmarsh Gifford. The double name had come into use early in the 14th century, perhaps because there was a need to distinguish it from Crowmarsh Battle [14]. The earl is also named in an inquisition of 1383, and in the Close Rolls of

1387, although in these two instances the earl was Laurence's grandson John, who died aged 17 in 1391 as a result of a jousting accident at Woodstock on Christmas Day. With John's death the manor presumably passed again to the Crown, but there is no further reference until the 17th and 18th centuries, when the name is always attached to that of Howbery, a Saxon name meaning 'hill spur manor'. By that time both names seem to refer to the same place. This suggestion is supported by a confirmation [15] from Henry VIII in 1510 to William Cope of a grant of free warren (in effect, a game licence) in Crowmarsh that had been given in 1346 by Edward III to a former lord, Ralph Restwold, whereas William refers in his will of 1513 to his manor of Howbery. Perhaps the name Howbery had gone out of use for a while after the Conquest. An inquisition of 1535, following the death of William's eldest son, Stephen, records that the manor was 'held of the Duke of Suffolk as of his manor of Ewelme' [16]. Among the manors listed in Quarter Sessions records of gamekeepers in the late 18th century, Howbery is named but not Crowmarsh Gifford.

Although Walter Giffard held the manor directly from the king, he enfeoffed, or sub-let, the manor to Hugh of Bolbec (near Le Havre), as is recorded in Domesday Book [17]. His grandson Walter of Bolbec is recorded in a charter of about 1181 as having the fee of Crowmarsh, which had been given to him by Henry II [18]. When he died in 1186 the enfeoffment passed to Robert of Vere, 3rd Earl of Oxford, who had married Walter's sister Isabel. The widowed countess is recorded as holding Crowmarsh in the Close Rolls of 1229 and 1230, the Kings Court Rolls of 1231, as well as in the Book of Fees and two charters of about that time among Wallingford records [19]. The manor stayed in the family until at least the 8th Earl of Oxford, Thomas, who died in 1371, when it had already been sub-let to Ralph Restwold [20]. It remained in the Restwold family until at least the mid 15th century. In the 17th and 18th centuries the 'manors or reputed manors of Howbery and Crowmarsh Gifford' (confusion over names seems to have been recognised even by then) passed through various hands [21]. They were acquired by Robert Nedham, of Bampton, about 1750 (judged by a poll book of 1754) and stayed in that family until they were sold in 1833 to William S. Blackstone by the executors of Robert's distant cousin, the Earl of Kilmorey (see Howbery Park). In 1858 the manors passed to Charles Hedges [22] and then to subsequent owners of Newnham Manor house. Today, they belong to Carmel College.

A charter of king Edgar, reputed date 966, describes the boundaries of Newnham estate [23]. Although some of the landmarks are impossible to identify, it does seem that there is some similarity with present-day Newnham. The description starts: 'From the heathen burial place up along the dyke to the boundary way. Up along the boundary way and then up to Watch Hill', and ends '. . . by the old way to the intermittent stream. After that along the intermittent stream to the Thames. Along the river to Catta's island'. The 'boundary way' can be equated with the road to Henley, from the Street up Crowmarsh Hill and Brixton Hill to Warren Hill, which in the early 18th century was called Warden Hill, meaning the same as Watch Hill - a look-out point [24]. Here, the estate boundary left the road, as has the boundary of Newnham parish for centuries since.

Returning to the start of the description, the parish boundary meets the Street opposite Crowmarsh Gifford church, having followed a ditch (perhaps the dyke mentioned) from the Thames. The heathen burial place has not been identified but would have been above flood level near Watery Lane. Having gone around the estate, the boundary came back downhill presumably following Grim's Ditch (curiously not mentioned, although it forms the southern boundary of Newnham parish for several miles), and certainly crossing Icknield Way (perhaps the 'old way'). There is still a small spring and stream on the parish boundary close to the Thames. Catta's island is stated (as Catteneyte - Catta's eyot) in a charter of

1377 as being on the south side of Wallingford bridge [25]. And so we return to near the start.

Estate boundaries were commonly marked by burial places of pagan Saxons [26], and one such place may be represented by the 16 skeletons found in 1947 beside Grims Ditch near Sheepcot [27].

At the time of Domesday, the manor of Newnham was held by Miles Crispin [17], but by the 13th century it was held of the king by Richard Morin for one knight's fee [28]. Both he and his son William gave lands there to Reading Abbey about 1220. The abbot rented out these lands for 5 marks (about £3) yearly until at least 1326 [29]. In that year the Fine Rolls record that the king ordered the manor to be delivered to Edmund of Bereford, following the death of his father, who had held it by the service of one knight's fee and the finding of two armed men for 40 days at Wallingford castle in time of war [30]. In 1340, Edmund complained that the parson of Mongewell, with others, had broken into his close and houses, carried away his goods, and assaulted his men and servants [31]. For a while, early in the 14th century, the manor was sometimes called Newnham-by-Wallingford or Newnham-by-Crowmarsh, but by the middle of that century it had come to be known as Newnham Murren [32], these names perhaps being used to distinguish the place from Nuneham Courtenay. In 1380, Edmund's grandson, Sir Baldwin of Bereford, was granted free warren by the king [33], but by 1428 the lands were held by Thomas Chaucer [14], son of the poet, Geoffrey. Thomas had been made Constable of Wallingford castle in 1399, and he represented Oxfordshire in Parliament several times from 1401 to 1430. After his burial at Ewelme in 1434, Newnham manor passed to his daughter Alice, wife of the Earl of Suffolk [34].

In 1519 the manor was leased by Henry VIII to Ralph Dean [15], and in 1565 and 1582 by Elizabeth I to her cousin John Fortescue [35], MP for Wallingford in 1572 and later Chancellor of the Exchequer. During the first half of the 17th century it was held by the Stonor family, but by 1685 it had passed to the Paul family, of Bray [36]. When Catherine Paul married in 1724 the manor passed to the Stapleton family, of Rotherfield Greys. Newnham Farm is recorded as being the manor house in 1772 [37]. Thomas Stapleton, Lord le Despencer, sold the manor in 1797 to Thomas Toovey [38], who may have started to extend the building now known as Newnham Manor house. It stayed in that family until 1855, when it was sold to Charles Hedges, who had married Thomas's granddaughter, Ann. After his death in 1902 the manor passed to successive owners of Newnham Manor house. It is curious that for much of the 18th century the name Newnham Warren was used [39].

In contrast to Crowmarsh and Newnham, it does seem that the lord of Mongewell lived at the manor house, although he was several steps down the feudal hierarchy. From the late 13th to the mid 14th centuries, the Loveday family held the manor [40]; and for much of the 16th and first half of the 17th centuries it was the Molins. When William Molins died in 1649 his trustees may well have sold the manor to pay his debts, for by 1660 it was in the hands of Thomas Saunders. Through the marriage of his granddaughter Jane it passed in 1731 to Sir John Guise, and then through the marriage of his daughter Jane it passed in 1783 to Shute Barrington, later bishop of Durham. Following his death in 1826, the manor passed successively to his great nephew Uvedale Price [41], and in 1845 to Uvedale's sister Dame Mary Ann Elizabeth Price, and then in 1878 to his cousin, General Edward Price [42]. When he died in 1888 the manor was sold to Alexander Fraser, and after his death in 1916 it came to Howard Gould (see Mongewell House).

The early history of North Stoke manor is obscure. Before the mid 14th century it was known either as simply Stoke(s) or as Stoke Basset, but after the mid 15th century these names were seldom used. The manor was held by the Basset family in the 13th century [43] and by the Moeles family in the 14th [44], but it is uncertain whether different parts were involved, even with parts of Ipsden. Subdivision certainly occurred later [45]. In 1604, the manor was described as 'Stokebasset otherwise Stokemules' [46]. By the late 18th century it had become part of the possessions of the lord of Mongewell, and it remained so until that estate was sold in 1918, North Stoke manor then passing to John Wormald of The Springs.

How many folk lived in the four villages of Crowmarsh? The 10-yearly censuses starting 1801 give us precise counts, and estimates for earlier years can be made from baptism records in parish registers. Crowmarsh Gifford provides the longest sequence. By comparing numbers of baptisms in 25-year periods with population from census returns we find that 100 baptisms in 25 years corresponds to a population of about 140. If we assume that this relation applies throughout the period of the registers then we can estimate population size since the late 16th century, although there is unfortunately a large gap centred on the early 18th century. The results are shown on the graph.

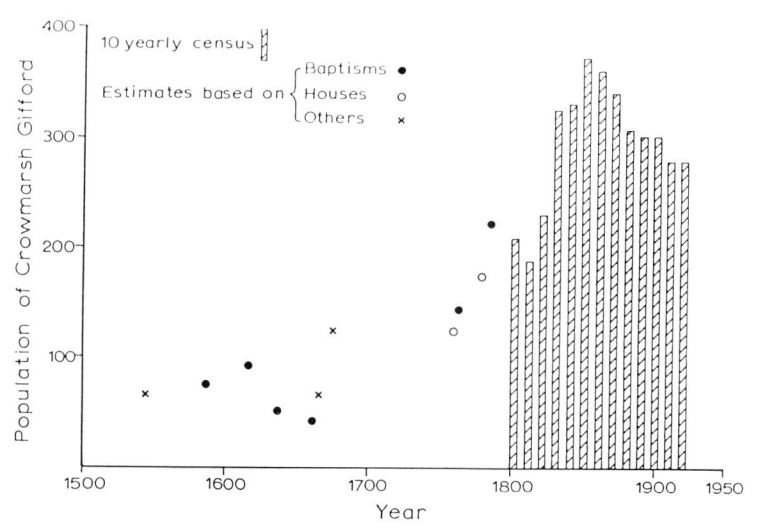

Change in population of Crowmarsh Gifford over four centuries.

It is possible to make further estimates from a few independent records. For example, the bishops' records for some years contain statements of the number of houses in the parish, and by comparing these with census records of the early 19th century we can judge that each house had about five occupants, on average. Extending this to the late 18th century, population estimates can be made in four years. Three further estimates can be made for

1676 from the Compton census of communicants, 87

1665 from the hearth tax returns, 14

1546 from the census of communicants, 42.

It is generally accepted that a multiplying factor of about 1.5 is needed for the two censuses, and of about 4 or 5 for the hearth tax returns. The resulting estimates, which have been added to the graph, are consistent with those derived from the baptism records and give us confidence that they are realistic.

Before 1600, all four villages had between 50 and 100 inhabitants each, but it is clear that the population of Crowmarsh Gifford increased five-fold to a maximum around the mid 19th century. The dip in the mid 17th century may be an effect of the civil war - either a real fall in population or a reflection of poor record keeping. The decline after 1850 probably indicates a fall off in numbers of farm workers as machinery was introduced. Similar but less pronounced trends occur with the other three villages, except that in Mongewell the population declined during the 18th century until about 1770. It seems that the estate was running down until bishop Barrington introduced considerable improvements in farming.

---

Opposite: occupations of heads of households, from the censuses 1841 to 1881.

*includes: letter carrier, strawbonnet maker, hay trusser, gravel digger, police constable, bricklayer, plasterer.

# Settlements

|  | 1841 | 1851 | 1861 | 1871 | 1881 |
|---|---|---|---|---|---|
| farmer/bailiff | 4 | 7 | 3 | 3 | 3 |
| labourer | 34 | 32 | 26 | 32 | 24 |
| shepherd | 0 | 0 | 2 | 3 | 3 |
| clergyman | 1 | 1 | 1 | 1 | 1 |
| publican | 1 | 1 | 1 | 1 | 1 |
| victualler/beerseller | 1 | 0 | 1 | 2 | 2 |
| schoolmaster | 0 | 0 | 0 | 0 | 1 |
| blacksmith | 2 | 0 | 1 | 1 | 1 |
| carpenter/wheelwright | 1 | 3 | 4 | 1 | 3 |
| shoemaker | 1 | 3 | 2 | 1 | 1 |
| tailor | 2 | 3 | 2 | 1 | 2 |
| engineer/machinemaker | 1 | 2 | 0 | 0 | 0 |
| iron founder | 0 | 0 | 0 | 1 | 1 |
| pipemaker | 1 | 1 | 1 | 1 | 0 |
| baker | 1 | 1 | 1 | 1 | 1 |
| shopkeeper/grocer | 1 | 3 | 1 | 1 | 1 |
| photographer | 0 | 0 | 0 | 0 | 1 |
| laundress | 1 | 1 | 0 | 1 | 2 |
| gardener | 0 | 2 | 3 | 3 | 3 |
| coachman | 0 | 0 | 0 | 1 | 1 |
| lodge keeper | 0 | 0 | 1 | 1 | 1 |
| groom | 0 | 0 | 0 | 0 | 1 |
| independent | 8 | 2 | 2 | 4 | 4 |
| others* | 3 | 9 | 18 | 16 | 17 |
| total | 63 | 71 | 70 | 76 | 75 |

The overwhelming domination of the land in providing employment is demonstrated for the 19th century by the occupations of heads of households recorded in the censuses. The table for Crowmarsh Gifford shows numbers under various headings at 10-year intervals from 1841 to 1881. Although labourers were by far the most numerous, their proportion fell from more than a half in 1841 to less than a third in 1881. The seven farms in 1851 perhaps reflect a lack of consolidation by the then principal landowner, the Revd Harry Lee, who had acquired much of the parish from his cousin William S. Blackstone [47]. In that year, Blackstone's house, Howbery Park, was unfinished. Gardeners were at work, but the lodge keeper, coachman and groom came later. The appearance of shepherds presumably reflects the interest in sheep breeding at Coldharbour by the de Mornays [48]. The traditional village craftsmen are present throughout. Note also the persistence of rector, publican, baker and shopkeeper; the demise of engineer and pipemaker; and the appearance of ironfounder, schoolmaster and photographer. All of these are discussed in a later chapter. Mongewell provides an interesting contrast. Whereas labourers were dominant, the proportion fell more rapidly than in Crowmarsh Gifford, perhaps because part of the land was taken out of farming to make a park. Again shepherds make their appearance, perhaps reflecting a trend away from arable. Apart from the carpenter-wheelwright there were no traditional craftsmen or shopkeepers because Mongewell was an estate parish, with estate workers such as gardeners, woodman and coachman.

Did village families stay on for many generations as is sometimes supposed? The answer generally is: no. Apart from a few exceptions, it is clear from surnames in parish registers that families often lasted only one or two generations. This implies widespread mobility, which is confirmed for the 19th century by the birthplaces recorded in the censuses. For example, of the 71 heads of households in Crowmarsh Gifford in 1851, 24 had been born there, six

Settlements                                          19

in Newnham Murren, Mongewell or North Stoke, 12 in Wallingford, and 29 elsewhere. In Newnham Murren, 30 of the 48 heads had been born elsewhere. This obvious mobility was not spread equally among the different occupations. Of the 34 labourer heads in Crowmarsh Gifford, 18 had been born there; but in contrast, of the 15 craftsmen and shopkeepers, only one had been born there. It seems that sons of farm workers tended to follow in their fathers' footsteps, whereas sons of those in village businesses moved away. Not many workers were as immobile as William King of North Stoke; he died in 1920, aged 68, having worked for 58 years on one farm [49].

The sites of North Stoke and Mongewell, clustered where streams from the perennial springs are strong enough to turn water mills yet set above all but the highest of Thames floods, contrast with the sites of Newnham Murren and Crowmarsh Gifford, stretched either side of a main highway. For about a hundred years, from the mid 18th century, Crowmarsh Gifford was in

Gardeners, early 20th century.

fact known also as Long Crowmarsh [50]. Why these two should have developed facing each other is unknown, but there are similar occurrences elsewhere in England. Perhaps Crowmarsh Gifford appeared after Newnham, with the granting of the manor to Walter Giffard. It has been claimed [51] that Newnham was at one time sited near the church and was moved as a consequence of the Black Death in 1348. However the little evidence available does not support that suggestion. For example, Reading Abbey charters of about 1220 imply that Newnham lay on the boundary of the Saxon estate [52], as it has lain on the northern boundary of the parish for centuries afterwards, because they refer to Newnham crofts (farm land enclosed near the houses) being near to Crowmarsh hospital, which must have been near the highway, as discussed on page 104. If Newnham did move to the main highway perhaps it was in early Norman times, as Wallingford's importance increased.

All four villages probably changed little in size from the time of Domesday to the end of the 18th century, although the available maps are on too small a scale to demonstrate it. Evenso, there is evidence of infilling or improvements, at least in Crowmarsh Gifford, from mentions of new buildings in deeds and wills. The buildings eastward from the former bakehouse illustrate houses and infillings at various times from about 1700. By mid 19th century, village extensions had been built: New Town at North Stoke, and Forest Row at Mongewell. Crowmarsh Gifford and Newnham Murren saw village renovations typical of the period: improvements to rectory and farms, and appearance of shops, schools and new houses. During the 20th century, with ever-improving agricultural technology, the need for farm workers' cottages dwindled, and farms not only grew larger by amalgamation but also became progressively less dependent on the villages. As a result both farm houses and workers' cottages were converted to private residences or were demolished to make way for new buildings. See also chapters 3 and 4. At the same time there was a growing need for new houses, but the First World War brought difficulties in finding sites and builders [53]. By 1920 it was agreed to put up six council houses near to the village hall in North Stoke, and ten next to the French Gardens, Benson Lane [54]. In 1942, 18 old cottages were unfit for habitation [55]. These included Dormer Cottages (at the corner of Lane End) and Retreat Cottages (next to the former Gamecock beerhouse), but it was not until the early 1970s that they were demolished and replaced. Meanwhile, in 1956, the Park View houses had been built, off Cox's Lane. A major housing expansion took place in 1967 when the Newnham Croft estate was started.

Dormer Cottages and Crowmarsh Farmhouse, about 1908.

# 2. The Land

Lying between Thames and Chilterns, Crowmarsh soils form a west-east progression, reflected in a variety of land uses. Close to the river, after winter floods the grass was mown in summer. Some of this meadow was common land, where villagers drew their portions yearly by lot - hence the early 18th century references to Lot Mead in North Stoke. Eastward from these meadows, the deep fertile soils of the lowest slopes for centuries have been cultivated for field crops; but the middle slopes, with their thinner chalky soils, were more suited to livestock. The upper slopes have a mantle of heavy clay with flints and, although areas have long been cultivated, there are still stretches of woodland that have almost certainly persisted since prehistoric times - sources of timber for building and of bark for Wallingford tanners. Spent tanbark was valuable for return to the land as mulch.

What crops did the farmers grow, and what livestock did they keep? For the 17th century, we can answer these questions by examination of wills' inventories - lists of parishioners' goods, compiled by friends and neighbours after death. From 26 such inventories it is clear that the principal cereals were wheat and barley, as they are today. Next came oats, and a few farmers grew rye or maslin (mixed cereals). Peas and vetches were the other main crops, the latter as fodder for animals. Hops and dills (for flavouring food) are also mentioned. In a similar analysis of 31 Crowmarsh inventories naming livestock, two thirds mentioned cows, and about one third listed pigs, horses, calves and sheep. Oxen were not mentioned at all; they had been replaced by horses as draught animals, probably during the previous century.

How was the land divided? 13th and 14th century references to Crowmarsh Field and Newnham Field suggest that much of the land in those two parishes during medieval times was in single common fields, where individual parishioners no doubt held one or more scattered strips or 'acres', as was common throughout England. By 1600 this system had been modified, for later records name several fields. For example, in Crowmarsh Gifford there are references to Stockbridge, The Hitchin and Crowbrook, all of which are Saxon names that had probably been used for parts, or furlongs, in the former Crowmarsh fields. 'Stokbruggforlonge' is named [1] in a deed of 1326. The timing of this modification into several fields is perhaps indicated by the ages of their boundary hedges. Using the well-known method of equating the number of woody species in a 30-yard section to the age in centuries, various hedges have been found to be about five centuries old, consistent with the Tudor emphasis on sheep enclosures. A shadow of the earlier layout of strips persists in the irregularities of the boundary hedge between the parishes of Crowmarsh Gifford and Benson, irregularities that elsewhere in England can be related to mapped strip patterns. Unfortunately there are no such maps for Crowmarsh, but several terriers, or lists of lands held by individual owners, show a system of strips being used. As well as in the open fields, some parishioners had strips in the Crofts, or croftland, bands of arable land behind the gardens on each side of the Street [2]. There are no references to Crowmarsh Crofts after the 17th century, but in Newnham Murren the name has persisted into this century, for a house called Newnham Croft was built on part of the land in 1903.

References to 'acres' cease in Crowmarsh Gifford wills and deeds after the 1760s, implying a change in the system of land holding. This can be related to the acquisition of the manors of Crowmarsh Gifford and Howbery by Robert Nedham about 1750. It is likely that he, or his son William, consolidated their farms so that the parishioners either sold their few acres or exchanged them for other land.

By 1763, a piece of land in Crowmarsh Gifford had come to be known as the Common, and from a map of 1872 this clearly is the same as the Marsh shown on the tithe map. It was a patch of wet pasture about half way along the north side of Marsh Lane, and presumably used by parishioners to keep a few cows, judged by the name Milking Path used for access across the Hitchin. This patch has now all but disappeared under Crowmarsh by-pass.

In contrast to Crowmarsh Gifford, there are very few references to 'acres' held by parishioners during the 17th and 18th centuries in the common fields of Newnham Murren and North Stoke, and no references even to common fields in Mongewell. It seems that the tradition of farming a few 'acres' by a proportion of the parishioners was most developed in Crowmarsh Gifford, whereas it did not exist at all in Mongewell. This contrast is no doubt related to differences in residence patterns by the lords of the manors. Whereas in Crowmarsh Gifford, Newnham Murren and North Stoke each lord had many lands elsewhere in England, and seldom or never resided in Crowmarsh, preferring to let their manor houses to others, by contrast the lord of Mongewell is known to have lived there back to at least 1600, and probably long before that. In North Stoke, 'acres' and furlongs persisted into the 19th century, for they are named in a terrier of glebe (the vicar's lands) for 1808. Also, a map of 1791 shows strips belonging to Rectory Farm, but the tithe map of 1848 shows no strips.

Little is known about farm sizes before the appearance of tithe maps and censuses in the mid 19th century. By then each parish had a few farms, of between about 100 and 700 acres, the largest being Newnham Farm. Even in 1606, Newnham Farm had 500 acres [3]. The censuses give the number of workers on each farm. It seems that one man was needed for about every 20 acres, or about 50 workers in each parish. In fact, 56 labourers are named in the 1851 census of Crowmarsh Gifford, almost all of whom can be taken as farm workers. Horses did the hard work, such as ploughing and carting, and 17th century inventories suggest that one horse was needed for about every ten acres of arable land. At that time, a horse was valuable - £2 6s - and a cow was valued at £2, but sheep were three or four to the £1.

Some land was set aside as garden allotments. Already by 1847 six acres between the Henley road and Hailey Way (Cox's Lane) were being used as such. For some unknown reason by the early 20th century these had come to be called Botany Allotments. In 1914 they were bought by Crowmarsh Gifford Parish Council for £200 (with a loan from the Public Works Loan Commissioners, to be paid back over 50 years), with Newnham Murren declining to join in because since 1911 they already had enough allotments - part of the Emery Charity lands, behind the Gamecock [4]. Ever since, Botany Allotments seem to have been more than ample to meet local needs, even when the government called in 1918 for more food to be grown. After the war many remained unlet, so in the mid 1930s land bordering the Henley road was sold for building plots. Evenso, by 1968 a half of the allotments were still unlet. With the opening of Port Way in 1987, the opportunity was taken to sell some of the allotments for building sites, at a price of nearly £500,000 - a remarkable increase since the sale of 1914!

Along the river bank, osiers - willow rods - were cut and peeled to be used for basket making. The name 'Rod Eyot', an example of which occurs in Crowmarsh, was often given to small islands with osier beds.

Besides the produce of the land there was fish to be had, both from the Thames, where fishing rights had been defined for centuries [5], and in the two mill ponds and other small ponds. In 1312 Newnham manor included a fishery in the Thames worth 6s 8d [6]; this 'ancient fishery' was mentioned still in the 1920 sale of the manor. In the early 19th century, Shute Barrington rented the water and fishing rights in the Thames, extending from Mongewell to Little Stoke, at £30 a year [7], and also kept his mill pond well stocked. An entry in his diary for 1793 proudly records that he had caught a 12lb pike in the pond [8]. Fisherman's Green, as the name suggests, is a small plot of land by the river at North Stoke now registered with the Charity Commissioners so that parishioners can fish there.

# 3. Farmers

Having looked at the land and how it was owned and farmed, we turn now to the farmers and their homes. With the increase in farm size this century, most of the former farmhouses have been converted to private residences, and some have been pulled down.

## Howbery Farm

It was here that Jethro Tull, the great improver of English agriculture, experimented in crop productivity. To economise in the use of scarce and expensive seed, he made the first drilling machine that worked [1]. Resistance by his farm hands was violent. In 1701, the year that his drill was made, Thomas Crane was brought to court in Oxford charged with assaulting Tull, and in the following year his servant Mary Willis confessed in court to allowing her master's goods to be stolen [2]. Persuaded by friendly and influential landowners, in 1733 Jethro's principles of fine tilth and weed control were published in his book 'Horse-hoeing husbandry', which in time led to a revolution in tillage methods.

Tull came to Howbery as a youth in the late 1680s. His father, also Jethro, 'of Crowmarsh, living at Howbery Farm' is recorded in 1691 as being elected to chief constable for the north division of Langtree hundred [1]. He is listed among the debtors of

THE

# Horſe-Hoing Husbandry:

OR, AN

# ESSAY

On the PRINCIPLES of

## TILLAGE and VEGETATION.

Wherein is ſhewn

A METHOD of introducing a Sort of *Vineyard-Culture* into the Corn-Fields,

In order to

Increaſe their Product, and diminiſh the common Expence;

By the Uſe of

INSTRUMENTS deſcribed in CUTS.

By *I. T.*

*Cum Privilegio Regiæ Majeſtatis.*

LONDON:

Printed for the AUTHOR, and Sold by G. *Strahan* in *Cornhill*; T. *Woodward* in *Fleet-Street*; A. *Miller* over-againſt St. *Clement's-Church* in the *Strand*; J. *Stagg* in *Weſtminſter-Hall*; and J. *Brindley* in *New-Bond-Street*.
MDCCXXXIII.

Title page of Jethro Tull's book, published 1733.

Farmers                                                          29

William Emery of Newnham Murren at the latter's death in 1690, but he had been living in Shalbourne, Berkshire in 1686. Two Tull burials at Crowmarsh Gifford, the second in December 1709, followed by the baptism of a daughter at Shalbourne in 1710 suggest that young Jethro left Howbery early in 1710, and this is consistent with the marriage in 1710 of a William Barrett 'of Howbery'. This William was parish constable of Crowmarsh Gifford from 1711 to 1713 [2]. William Wilmot was at Howbery Farm in 1712; his will of 1717 shows that he was a wheelwright. During the 1720s, Isaac Allibone lived at Howbery [3]. In 1729, one of his turkeys (worth 10d) was stolen by John Westall. He had been seen hiding it in a ditch [2]. The Allibones may have continued at Howbery until the 1730s, for Isaac's wife was buried in Crowmarsh

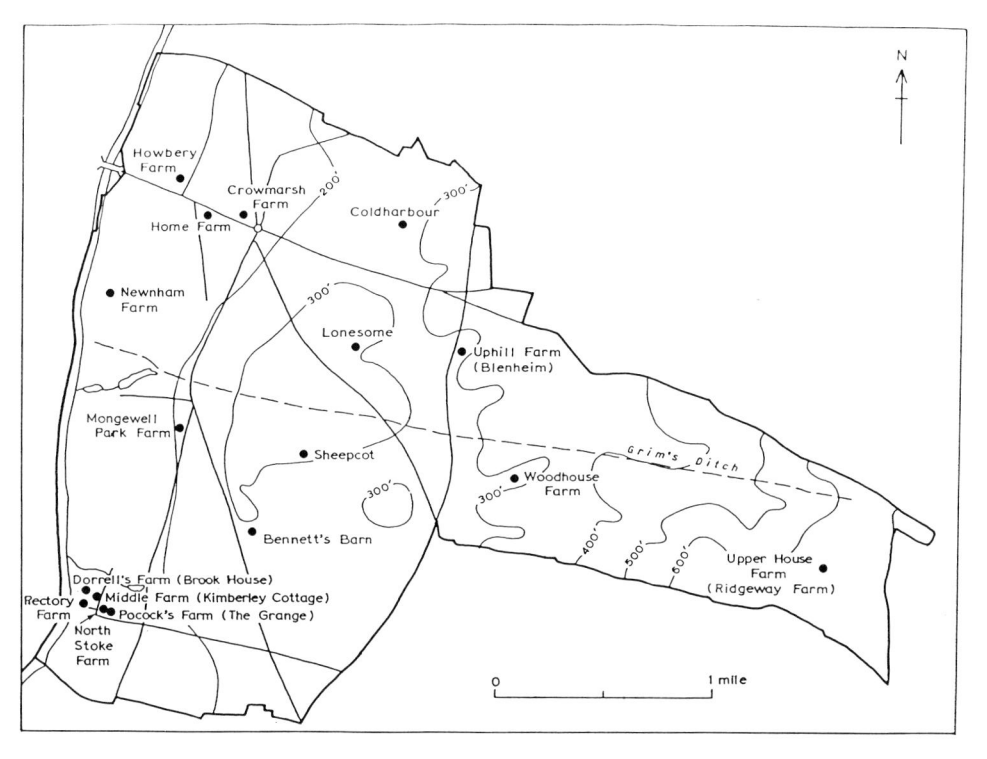

Farmhouses in the 1840s.

Gifford in 1737. The last farmer known to be 'of Howbery' was Richard Keats, a yeoman according to his will of 1746. He was in court at Oxford at least three times [2]: in 1738 charged with assaulting Elizabeth, the wife of Joseph Chester; in 1739 for not providing a jury list, one of the duties of parish constable; and in 1740 for uttering four oaths. Richard seems to have been a prickly character!

The name 'Howbery', referring to the farmhouse, can be traced back to at least the mid 16th century. William Cope of Ashton, Northamptonshire, in his will of 1558, refers to his 'manor place or chief capital mansion house of Howbery, in the county of Oxford . . now or late in the occupation of John Stoner, esquire . . . . and let to farm'. John Stonor had lived at Rectory Farm, North Stoke, and his eldest daughter, Margaret, had married about 1540 William Hildesley, who was living in Crowmarsh Gifford in 1546, according to a tax return for that year [4]. In his will dated

1920s street scene, showing one of the original gas lamps outside old Howbery Farmhouse.

2 March 1576 William bequeathed 'half of my farm of Howbery which I hold for 30 years from Michaelmas last' to his wife, and the other half to his eldest son Walter. The family were Roman Catholics and were fined for their recusancy [5]. By 1592 Walter had moved to another family home at East Ilsley, Berkshire, and he died there in 1596, but his brother William continued at Howbery until at least 1603, and perhaps until the lease ran out in 1605. Certainly by 1613 he had moved to Little Stoke, but died at East Ilsley in 1622. Their sister Cicely married Walter Bigg of Crowmarsh Gifford and became grandmother of Walter Bigg, founder of Wallingford School. There is a brass memorial to the Hildesley family in Crowmarsh Gifford church.

What was the farmhouse like? More than 20 records dated from 1558 to 1746 refer either to Howbery or Howbery Farm. One of these records, a list of householders summoned to appear for the Visitation of Berkshire by the Heralds of the College of Arms in 1665-6, states that William Loader senior dwelt at Howbery, and the hearth tax returns for 1665 give William Loader as paying for ten hearths, the most of any house in Crowmarsh Gifford [6]. Several mid 17th century records refer to a 'capital messuage or farm' leased along with the manor, from which we can infer that the farmhouse was also the manor house [7]. An undated rental (of about 1715, judged by internal evidence) describes the manor house as 'containing nine rooms on a floor', with 'two large barns, a stable to hold twelve horses, carthouse, pigeonhouse and other necessary buildings, two orchards of two acres, fish ponds, meadow, pasture and arable lying and being contiguous to the house, containing by estimation 105 acres, let to Richard Wilkins at £110 p.a.'[8]. One of the mid 17th century records also describes Howbery as having a pigeonhouse. Note that Howbery Farm was being leased in all these records, and the same would have been true at the time of Jethro Tull.

None of these records enables us to place the farmhouse within the village, but later records do. A deed of 1763 lists, among property in the parish sold by the executors of Elizabeth Cottingham (a great-granddaughter of Walter Bigg), to William (later Sir William) Blackstone of Wallingford, a 'messuage . . , malthouse, barn, stable . . . . and pigeonhouse', south of Barbican Close and in the occupation of John Allnatt [9]. (John had come as a boy from North Stoke about 1743 with his father Richard, who probably took Howbery Farm after the Richard Keats already mentioned.) This description is similar to that of Howbery manor house, although a malthouse is mentioned for the first time, and no other farm is known to have had both malthouse and pigeonhouse. Its position can be determined with certainty because it stayed in the Blackstone family for two more generations. A land tax exemption certificate of 1799 describes it as 'a messuage used as three tenements in the occupation of John Allnatt, John Cummins and widow [Mary] Parker', property of Henry Blackstone (William's son) [10]. These three dwellings correspond to a house and two cottages in the 1845 schedule accompanying the tithe award map, and they are still standing just west of Wilder's foundry. The cottages were occupied by Charles Blissett and Elizabeth Read, although previously (according to a mortgage indenture of 1872 [9]) by William Read (known to have been the husband of Elizabeth) and Ann Cummins, widow (presumably of John). A further piece of evidence comes from a sketch map with a 1770 lease of lands just west of the building, which are shown as two orchards, Burchs and Clacks [11]. The only known person in Crowmarsh with a name like Burchs was Francis Burgess, who was described as 'of Howbery' when he was married in 1678 at Ipsden.

The building as it stands today has a frame of substantial timbers, the earliest part consisting of four bays built at the same time, together with an extension at the west end in a similar style. The whole would allow for ten rooms, consistent with the hearth tax record, but all the 17th century chimneys seem to have been replaced, suggesting that the frame was built before chimneys were integral parts of a small manor house, and perhaps in the 16th century or earlier. Another extension, of brick, was added around 1700. It is easy to see how the building could be divided into separate dwellings, as it is now. This may have happened as early as the mid 18th century, for the Richard Keats already mentioned describes himself in his will of 1746 as 'of Upper Howbery'.

But why was the house no longer associated with the manor when it was sold in 1763? After Robert Nedham acquired the manor, about 1750, his newly-built mansion would have become the manor house. He did not buy Howbery farmhouse because after John Cottingham had bought it, by 1738, the executors of his widow, Elizabeth, did not sell it until 1763, as we have already noted. Perhaps Isaac Allibone, last known to have been at Howbery in 1730 [2], sold the manor to William Smith (who in turn is known to have sold the house to the Cottinghams) and the land to Nedham, who turned part of the estate into a park and built a new farmhouse at Coldharbour.

Another new farmhouse was also built in Benson Lane and came to be known as Howbery Farm. It bears the date 1770 and carved initials IA and MA, referring to John and Mary Allnatt. Later, John Kitchen was the farmer, followed by his son James, but the house had become a private residence by the time of the 1881 census.

Meanwhile, the western part of the old building remained as a farmhouse until the mid 19th century, when it was known as the Dairy House, and the eastern part continued as cottages, with its Tull connections forgotten [10].

## Crowmarsh Farm

Although the name 'Crowmarsh Farm' did not come into use until late in the 19th century (for example, it does not appear before then on maps or in census returns), the house can be recognised in much earlier records. At the sale of 1833, its position is shown on a map, and the homestead is described as 'a brick-built and tiled farmhouse with four bedrooms, parlours, kitchen . . . cellars . . . stable . . . barn' [12]. This description corresponds fairly well with the rooms and buildings listed in four inventories: of Richard Arthur 1725, Richard Butler 1679, William Sadler 1662 and Thomas Clack 1614. The house has 1692 in its brickwork, which is consistent with its description in a rental of about 1710: 'a new-built brick house with barns, stables . . . .' [8]. Presumably 'new-built' meant 'newly modified', for only two rooms had been added by the time of the 1725 inventory. Letters in the brickwork, I$^B$A (which can be mistaken for I$^D$A) are presumably those of the occupiers at the time.

Crowmarsh Farmhouse, with 'IBA' or 'IDA' in the brickwork.

The inventory of William Sadler includes the 'parsonage barn', or tithe barn, which is known to have been part of Crowmarsh Farm because it is shown there on the tithe map of 1841 and confirmed by the church rates on the tithe barn from 1854 onwards paid by Joseph Moores [13], who is named at Crowmarsh Farm at the time of the 1861 census. In the sale of 1833, there was a 'brick-built and thatched 5-bay barn', corresponding to a 5-bay barn in a terrier of church lands dated 1685 [14].

So Crowmarsh Farm can be traced back with some confidence to at least 1614; but what do we know about the farmers? The Clacks had been farmers in Crowmarsh for several generations. Andrew Clack, who died in 1568, described himself as a 'husbandman', which can be taken to mean a small, independent farmer. He bequeathed three cows, three bullocks and 28 sheep to his four sons and two daughters, as well as 20 quarters of barley. Taking an average yield of about four quarters to the acre, this implies that Andrew had at least five acres of arable land. Indeed, his will refers to three 'yardlands', equivalent to at least 45 acres, as well as other lands. His estate passed to his eldest son, Thomas Clack, yeoman, who at his death in 1614 had nearly 70 acres planted (mostly barley and wheat, but some rye, oats, vetches and dills) as well as six horses, four hoggs, two cows and three calves.

Thomas Clack was a kindly man. He left one of his houses to the tenant, widow Margaret Bartholomew, for life, at 12s a year, and then to his servant Robert Tucker for 21 years. He ordered that his young nephew, Thomas Cheyney, whose father had died ten years previously, 'shall be suffycientlye kept with meat and drink and cloths at the cost and charges of my executors untill he shall accomplyshe the age of xiiij years'. He also gave 12d to each of 14 poor householders in the parish. Thomas Clack had no children, and he handed on the farm firstly to his wife Joyce and brother William, and secondly to his nephew John, on condition that John became a partner with Joyce or William, whichever should live the longer. Perhaps this condition hints at Thomas having some foresight of likely trouble ahead, for John ran into debt. Although John was the second highest taxpayer at the time of the 1642 lay subsidy [15], implying a substantial estate still, in his will of 1668 he does not mention the house, only two other, smaller tenements. He had probably left Crowmarsh Farm, for William Sadler had come there before 1662. John's son, Matthew Clack, had to pay off remaining debts [16]. In 1670 he sold 48 acres to David Bigg of Wallingford [16], son of Walter; and in the same year he mortgaged one of the small tenements to William Emery (see page 111)[16]. It seems that John's debts were considerable, and much of the family estate had to be sold. Incidentally, Matthew's brother William was the first man known to have had the Queens Head, at the end of the 17th century.

We know little about the occupants following John Clack. William Sadler, yeoman, had been living at Newnham Murren in 1646, and his widow paid tax on only one hearth in 1665, so presumably she had moved out of the farmhouse, which can be expected to have had more than one hearth [6]. From an account drawn up after William's death we discover that administration of his estate cost £1 5s 3d. The funeral expenses of Richard Butler, a glover, were £1 15s, and the proving of his will cost £1 6s. He owed more than £150, including £50 to his son John, who had married the daughter of another Crowmarsh glover, Francis Foster, himself owed £3 6s for gloves by Walter Bigg at his death in 1659 [17]. It wasn't uncommon for death to catch up with debts! And why were there two glovers living in Crowmarsh at this time? Presumably they both traded in Wallingford.

Richard Arthur came to Crowmarsh about 1710, probably from Nuffield, where he had a house. He was living in Crowmarsh Gifford in 1711, and was elected parish constable in 1713 [2]. In his will of 1725 he says he had bought his Crowmarsh house from a Mr Townson, and he bequeathed it first to his son Hugh, and after Hugh's death to his grandson Richard. But this was on condition that 'my loving wife Joyce shall have the use of the parlour and the chamber over it with the gardens thereto belonging . . . . with the use of two beds and other goods for her conveniancy dureing her naturall life for her and her daughter Mary to live in, with liberty to make a doorway through the stone wall to go into the same parlour without the lett or disturbance of my son Hugh or any other person or persons whatsoever'. Grandson Richard was also given a piece of an orchard on which to build a house. This orchard lay on the opposite corner of what is now Lane End. In 1733, Hugh Arthur leased it to William Higgs of Newnham Murren [18], and it came to be known as Arthur's Orchard.

Hugh Arthur died in 1758, and Richard apparently in 1775. Perhaps it was about then that John Allnatt became the farmer, the house having probably been already sold to William Nedham of Howbery. John Allnatt is named as occupier in the land tax returns that start in 1786, along with James Woodley from 1820 to at least 1832 [19]. By 1845 the occupiers were Mary Allnatt, widow (presumably John's), and James Kitchen (of Howbery Farm). Then came Daniel Alderman, from Mackney, followed by Joseph Moores, already mentioned. But after he left (about 1862) there were several bailiffs until Henry Langford came in 1894 at the invitation of the owner, Alfred de Mornay. Henry had been shepherd on the de Mornay estate for many years, living in the cottage at the bend in Clack's Lane [20]. He stayed until 1908, when the farm was acquired by John W. Edwards at his marriage. By 1921, farming had become centred at Home Farm, Newnham Murren, and the house was divided into two residences. Today it is called Fernleigh.

## Coldharbour

Although now the largest in Crowmarsh, this farm has not had a long history. The earliest known reference to Coldharbour, or Coldharbour Farm, is Jefferey's 1766 map of Oxfordshire [21]. At the sale of 1833 the farm was let to William Parsons (at £344 a year) [12], and he is recorded in the land tax returns from 1788, preceded by Benjamin Parsons in 1786. Coldharbour is not named as such in those returns. It had probably been built shortly before the new Howbery Farm (1770) by William Nedham, as both farms were then on his land. Howbery was perhaps the 'home farm', near Howbery House, and Coldharbour a new place set in the midst of a large field recently converted from strip cultivation (page 24). Such isolated farms are a feature of the Oxfordshire countryside. Why the name was chosen we do not know.

At the sale of 1833, Coldharbour was bought by Robert Mayne Clarke, a surgeon in Wallingford [9]. He made improvements, for a barn bears the inscription 1843 RMC, but it seems he did not move in for some time because he was still in Wallingford Market Place

Harvest home.  Coldharbour, about 1900.

in 1847.  In the next year he converted the farmhouse from one with four groundfloor rooms and five bedrooms into a gentleman's residence with eight groundfloor rooms and 12 bedrooms.  It seems he needed the space, for at the 1851 census his household included seven children and nine servants.  Pencil drawings of hunting scenes on the walls of former stables are dated 1855 and signed RGC.

Farming in mid 19th century was carried on by a bailiff, Crowmarsh-born Moses Pauling, until Robert's widow, Ann, sold Coldharbour in 1862 to Edward de Mornay of Howbery House, for about £15,000 [22].  The property passed to his brother Alfred, who preferred to name the house Col d'Arbres.  He was a typical Victorian squire, distant from his employees [19], but known for his experiments to improve both the Southdown breed of sheep and the yield of cereal crops.  Among later owners was Sir Cecil Harcourt-Smith, one-time Director of the Victoria and Albert Museum, and an adviser to king George V for the royal art collection [23].

Bailiffs continued at Coldharbour until 1908, when John W Edwards took over the farming, first from Crowmarsh Farm and later from Home Farm, Newnham Murren.  His son, John T Edwards, moved to Coldharbour when he bought it in 1944.

### Newnham Farm

For centuries Newnham Farmhouse had been the manor house of Newnham Murren [24], but the lord of the manor almost never lived there.  It was occupied by tenant farmers until 1980, when it was sold as a private residence by the then owners, Carmel College.

The earliest known occupier was Richard Dean, in 1565 [25], although the manor had been leased in 1519, at £13 6s 8d yearly, to Ralph Dean, perhaps a forebear [26]. Among later occupiers were Edward Skinner and Francis Mercer, who died in 1582 and 1589 respectively, both having had the same wife, Lettice.

She outlived a third husband, Francis Barnard, as her brass memorial in Newnham Murren church records.

The farm was leased by Elizabeth I to (Sir) John Fortescue in 1565 and again in 1582. A survey of the farm in 1606 mentions a garden and orchard, and describes the dwellinghouse as tiled, as was the greater part of the wheat barn [27]. Earlier, in 1362, the value was 2s yearly for the house, a garden and two acres of pasture, together with 33s 4d for 100 acres of arable land 'below the hill' and 40d for 40 acres 'on the hill', as well as 20s for ten acres of meadow, 6s 8d for 20 acres of heathland, and 4s for the fishery [28].

Edward Cliff was the tenant in 1616, when the 'housing, hedges, mounds and fences . . . . were become, through the bad husbandry of the former tenants, very ruinous and in great decay . . . . and lands grown out of heart'. The then lord of the manor, Edward Winter, wished to raise the rent from the £100 yearly it had been for some time but he 'could not find any man to deal with him'. However, he did lease it to Edward Cliff in 1611 for 31 years, at £100 yearly, because Cliff had been put to trouble and expense on Winter's behalf, and anyway had married Winter's sister![29]

By 1685, Anthony Day was the farmer [30]. He had come to Newnham Murren between the time of the hearth tax returns of 1665 and his first mention in the parish registers in 1678. His son was a principal contender in the extended litigation over the will of William Emery (page 112).

Thomas Toovey acquired the farm in 1797 [11], but probably had a bailiff to work the land. The next known farmer was Charles Fuller, who came about 1845, when he is first mentioned in the parish registers. By 1892 he had retired and moved to Bournemouth, but he was buried at Newnham in 1909. He was followed by John Manley who, despite having blown off his left arm with a gun in an accident as a boy of 12, was an excellent shot and usually excelled all others at the annual rook shoot [20]. His wife tried to introduce the ideas of the Plymouth Brethren to Newnham. He left in 1904 to become a beekeeper [31].

The name **Lonesome** has been used since at least 1841 for a homestead long occupied by workers from Newnham Farm. It had been built, perhaps in the late 18th century, about a mile away, presumably for easy access to the more distant fields; hence its name. By 1913 it was being worked with Home Farm.

**Blenheim** has been the name of another homestead since the late 19th century, but for much of that century it had been called Uphill Farm or Upper Lonesome, and before about 1800 it was known as Newnham Wood [32]. The place has been referred to from at least the early 17th century as a separate part of Newnham Farm, but when the first buildings were set up is not known, although it is shown on a map of 1766 [21].

### Home Farm

The modern houses called 'Home Farm' were built in 1968 on the site of an old farmstead. This had come to be known by the mid 19th century as Creswell's Farm [32] because Thomas Creswell had lived there from about 1720 until his death in 1773. He is recorded as having been a churchwarden from 1743 to 1764 [33], and parish constable in 1755 [2]. A 1761 fire policy with the Sun Insurance Company covered the farmhouse, stable and barn for £300 [34]. When the farm had been sold in 1757 to William Toovey of Wallingford it was part of the property known as Brownch [11], and may well have been called that from at least the start of the 18th century, when the owner, Bartholomew Smith, had died. He, and before him his father, another Bartholomew, were probably the owners from at least 1642, when a Bartholomew Smith is named in a lay subsidy return for Newnham Murren [15]. Farmers before Creswell are unknown; presumably one is among those inhabitants named as paying hearth tax in 1665,

*A true Inventory of all the Goods and Chattells of John Roberds late of Newnham Murren in the County of Oxon Husbandman Deced Taken and Appraised by John Higgs and Richard Arthur the fifth Day of December Anno Dni 1711*

| | |
|---|---|
| His wearing Apparrel & ready money | 09 – 10 – 0 |
| In the Barne, 6 Bush: of Wheat 8 Bush: of Barley, a Sive Riddin rake & fork | 02 – 19 – 0 |
| Stallyoar & boards | 00 – 18 – 0 |
| In the Backside, one Cow | 03 – 00 – 0 |
| a Wheel barrow whitels, wood & other odd things | 00 – 06 – 0 |
| In the Kitchin, Brass pewter, 2 Spitts, 1 pair of Dogs fire shovel Tongues gridiron and other iron ware | 03 – 01 – 0 |
| One Long Table 3 Joyn Stools, 2 Chairs, 1 old Cupboard salt box with other odd things | 00 – 12 – 0 |
| In the Ground Chamber, a flock bed bedsteadle bedding 1 Long Table 2 Coffers 2 Chairs 1 box one Chest & other odd things | 03 – 00 – 0 |
| Three pair of Sheets 4 pillow beers towels & napkins | 01 – 01 – 0 |
| In the Upper Chamber an old flock bed bedstead and bedding & 2 old Coffers | 00 – 16 – 0 |
| In the Buttery, 4 Barrells 3 Tubbs 2 Kivers 1 Stand 1 powdring Tubb & other odd things | 01 – 08 – 0 |
| In the Shop 1 Tubb 3 Sarks & some old Lumber | 00 – 12 – 0 |
| In the Coffers 9 Bush: of Beans | 01 – 00 – 3 |
| Barley 10 Bushels sold | 02 – 00 – 0 |
| In the field, 1 Acre of Wheat | 00 – 16 – 0 |
| In Debts good & bad | 72 – 00 – 0 |
| | 95 – 19 – 3 |

Appraised by us

John Higgs

Richard R Arthur
His mark

A list of the goods that John Roberds, husbandman (small-holder), of Newnham Murren, had at his death in 1711, drawn up on 5 December by his neighbours John Higgs (who signs his name) and Richard Arthur (who makes his mark). The goods were worth £95–19s–3d, of which £72 were debts owing. (Oxfordshire Archives.)

but there is not enough evidence to tell which [6]. The Stamps may have been occupiers in the 16th century.

From just before Creswell's death it seems that William Absolon was the farmer, until he died in 1818. Then there was a succession of bailiffs, working first to the owner, William Toovey and later Thomas Toovey, and then to the farmers at Newnham Farm. When William H. Herbert bought the Newnham estate in 1902 the name Home Farm was already in use [35], presumably because it was close to Newnham House and to distinguish it from the more distant Newnham Farm. By 1907, John Rowden was the farmer, then Henry Cook until 1921, when John W. Edwards bought it and lived there [31].

## Mongewell Park Farm

This farm, along with Woodhouse and Upperhouse, was part of the Mongewell estate until that was split up at the sale in 1918. After Shute Barrington acquired the estate in 1770 he put much effort into improving it. He even had a threshing mill worked with two horses, costing 50 guineas. His diary records much detail about dates of sowing and harvesting, and the effects of weather on yield. As well as improving the farms he built six pairs of workers' cottages in the 1790s, including two at Mongewell Park Farm, one at Sheepcot and one at Upperhouse [36]. They provided good accommodation, well in advance of their time, and some are still standing although more or less modified. His great nephew, Uvedale Price, built two more pairs in a similar style at Forest Row in 1831.

Little more than the names of the farmers is known, and only from about the mid 18th century [37]. In the mid 19th century, Joseph Clarke, from the North Stoke mill family, was at Mongewell Farm, as it was known until recently, but by 1851 he had returned to the mill, presumably following the death of his father in 1848, and his brother Robert took over the farm.

44                    Farmers

In 1861 he had 280 acres, with 10 labourers and four boys. Following his widow's death in 1872, George Cottrell became the farmer, but after his death in 1874 there are no further references to farmers, perhaps because the estate was sold in 1878 to Alexander Fraser [38], who presumably came to rely on his bailiff at Woodhouse Farm to look after both. The oldest part of the building is Tudor, but it was added to in the 17th century. A pillar in the barn is marked 1641.

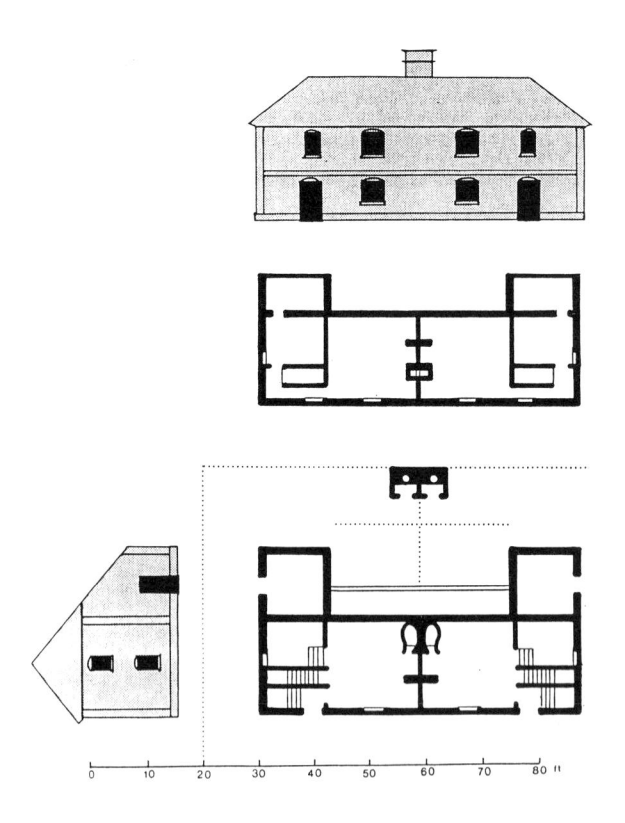

Plan of Barrington's cottages for his farm workers, about 1780.                              From Young 1813.

## Woodhouse Farm

This was part of the Mongewell estate until that was sold and broken up in 1918, when Glynn Williams of Hailey bought the farm for £9,300 [39]. Little is known about the farmers. Members of the Dodd family were there in the 18th century [37] - Matthew from at least 1757 to about 1770, and John from about 1780 to 1802, when he moved to Garsons, Ipsden, and later Wellplace. The last tenant farmer was James Painter, from about 1840 to about 1882, after which there were bailiffs.

## Upper House Farm

Before the mid 19th century this was more often called simply Upper Farm [37], but now it is Ridgeway Farm, and the name has been transferred to the former farm cottages. Like Woodhouse, it used to be part of the Mongewell estate. John Cooper was the tenant from 1767 to 1805, but little is known about him or later farmers.

## Brook House

This fine old house has been a private residence since early this century, but before then it was the house of Dorrell's Farm, named after four generations of Robert Dorrell who had lived there for about a hundred years. We don't know when the first Robert came to North Stoke, but his will of 1662 shows that the farm was then called Burghfield, a name that appears earlier, in terriers of 1600 and 1584 [40]. On the south side of the house is a small walled garden with a stone tablet inscribed 'Bilt in the year 1657. Here stands the letters of my Father and Mother. RD 1657. Robert Dorrell the younger laid this stone May 15'. On the east wing a date stone marked 1675 RD shows that this Robert extended the house, as can be confirmed by comparing the rooms named in his probate inventory of 1703 with those in the inventory of his father, dated 1662. The rooms had increased from seven to 13, including two garrets that had apparently been put in the roof space. It was probably the third generation Robert who put up the sundial on the south-west corner of the church tower when it was rebuilt in 1725.

The fourth Robert died in 1753, and his widow Elizabeth in 1761 married her neighbour William Allnatt, of what is now Kimberley Cottage [41], so perhaps the house passed to him and then to John Bennett, who seems to have married William's daughter, Martha, and was at the farm by 1789 [19]. Despite being a leading farmer in the parish, like others John did have his awkward moments. In 1806, for example, five of his pigs were impounded by Thomas Dodd of North Stoke Farm for damaging the latter's peas and beans in the common fields![2]. Three generations of Bennetts prospered at Dorrell's Farm for over a hundred years, enabling them to build an additional farmstead in the mid 19th century, Bennett's Barn, by the Reading Road opposite the end of Wix Way, but now it is pulled down.

About 1910, when the farmhouse had come to be known as Brook House, Harold Hartley came there on retirement [42]. He had been a publisher, founder of the Burlington Magazine, and director of several exhibitions in London. After receiving the Military Cross in 1916 [43], at the age of 65, he bought the house in 1919 [44] and lived there until his death in 1943. In 1939, Hartley's biography 'Eighty eight not out' was published.

From the mid 19th century until the sale in 1919 Dorrell's Farm was the manor house of North Stoke [45]. Previously the owner had been Charles Slater, a London brewer, who had married Mary the daughter of the last Robert Dorrell [41], so perhaps the later Dorrells had come to own the farm, although the first was certainly a tenant, as shown by his will of 1662.

## Kimberley Cottage

In 1580, Sir John Arundel sold his property in North Stoke to St John's College, Oxford, including a house called Goldes with 'stable and barn, two little closes of half acre each with hedgerows of elm, 35 acres arable, one acre mead' [46]. The tenant, Thomas Whichelo, could keep 40 or 60 sheep, three beasts and four horses, all at the yearly rent of 24s 6d. The house of this small farm corresponds to Kimberley Cottage of today, which may well contain parts of the 16th century building.

In 1628, Thomas's granddaughter Jane married Richard Allnatt of Ipsden, and in 1637 he acquired the lease, becoming the first of eight generations of Allnatts to be farmers there [47]. For much of the 18th century the rent was '19s 8d, one bushel one peck one pottle of wheat, and 14 bushels of malt'. The last of the line was a William Parsons Allnatt, who died childless in 1868. His widow, Sarah, stayed on, letting the land for about £80 a year, but she died in 1884. In her time the house was called Middle Farm, presumably because it lay between Dorrell's Farm to the north and Rectory Farm to the south. Census returns, and a list of landowners in 1873, show that the farm had about 40 acres - remarkably little change in 300 years. In 1617 this had been called a 'yardland' [48]. The land was sold by St John's College in 1895, and the house in 1905 (for £250), since when it has been a private residence [49].

## Rectory Farm

Originally this was the parsonage for the rector of North Stoke, but after the rectory was granted in 1391 to Bromhall Priory the house was leased to a succession of tenants [50]. This scheme continued after Henry VIII suppressed the Priory in 1521 and granted the rectory to St John's College, Cambridge, in the following year [51]. In 1529 the lease passed to John Stonor for a yearly rent of £15 together with five marks (about £3) to the College of St Nicholas in Wallingford Castle, and 6s 8d to the bishop of Lincoln for a pension [52]. The house then stayed with this branch of the Stonor family until 1602, when William Molins of Mongewell manor acquired the lease [53]. William Dormer took over in 1632, but no doubt he sublet, for in 1669 William Harbert was living there. The inventory of his goods, dated 1672, lists seven rooms downstairs and three upstairs (including a 'blue chamber'), corresponding well with the nine hearths on which he paid tax in 1665.

The Priory, and later the College, provided a vicar who, in 1425, was granted the manse and gardens. He seems to have had a place in the house, for about 1530 the vicarage was described as being in great decay and unable to be mended because 'it stands upon [the College's] house' [54]. This curious description is explained by an agreement of 1548 which states that the upper part of the south end of the house used to be the vicar's lodging. The house was then said to be 'wasted and decayed' [55]. Although it was no doubt improved by the Stonors, for it was clearly in good condition when William Harbert lived there, the house deteriorated again. A terrier of 1790 describes it as 'very large, built of brick and lath and plaster, tiled, the roof tolerably good, the inside very ruinous but is now repairing . . . . inhabited by four poor families'. There was then also 'a large barn with two floors for threshing lately laid new and part of the barn rebuilt, the whole in good repair', as well as a pigeonhouse, 'an octagon, part brick and lath and plaster, tiled, new built about five years since' [56]. Both barn and pigeonhouse still stand.

From 1820 John King, from Harwell, was the tenant, farming about 250 acres. His son, John Pittman King, continued until his death in 1920, when the house was sold to Sir John Wormald, of The Springs. The following year he linked it to his electricity generator at North Stoke mill [39]. It then became a private residence: first for Charles Crump, father of Neville Crump, trainer of three Grand National winners; and from 1945 for Donald Trentham. After his death the house was bought in 1984 by actor Michael Caine.

## The Grange

Nothing is known about this house before the late 18th century, when it was called Pocock's Farm [57], presumably after one Pocock who is known to have been a landowner in the 1760s [58]. He may have been the Henry Pocock named in 1737. By 1795 it had been bought by Francis King, but farmed successively by his sons Isaac and John, the latter also having Rectory Farm. In the mid 19th century it became a private residence, at first divided into two. The present name came into use about 1880. In the 1920s, one owner, a Mrs Briggs, kept lions there and used to take them for a walk down the Street!

## North Stoke Farm

In the 16th and 17th centuries, several generations of the Bristow family farmed here [59], but from the mid 18th century the Dodd family had the lease, from the Morrells of Moulsford. Thomas Dodd was churchwarden for several years. When he died in 1803 the farm passed to his nephew, another Thomas, son of his brother John Dodd of Ipsden, followed by his great nephew, yet another Thomas, and finally to the latter's widow, Mary. She carried on farming the 500 acres and more until 1882, aged 79, after giving notice to quit because her request for a reduction in rent had been refused [60]. In that year the farm was sold by the Morrells to Robert Keen [61], and his son Charles sold it again in 1938 [62], when a grandson, also a Robert Keen, kept some of the buildings where he made various kinds of farm vehicles, including the 'North Stoke Waggon' and 'Keen's Tractor Cart'. In 1962 the farm was sold to David Allen [63].

# 4. Houses

From manor houses to cottages, Crowmarsh has a range of home styles, some of them with histories going back more than two centuries, as the following accounts relate.

### Mongewell Park

Among the buildings comprising Carmel College is a large brick mansion in William-and-Mary style known as Mongewell Park [1]. It was finished in 1890 for Alexander Fraser, whose initials and the year 1889 can be seen on the lodge gates. When Fraser died in 1916 the house became a hospital for officers wounded in the First World War, but in 1918 it was sold to an American millionaire, Howard Gould. He was an atheist who made the path to Mongewell church sunken so that he could not see the users. After he sold the house, in 1939, the Royal Air Force occupied it until 1945, the lawns becoming cluttered with wooden huts [2]. The house then remained damaged and empty until Carmel College bought it in 1953 [3]. New buildings were then added piecemeal: the spectacular synagogue was opened in 1964; a sports building the next year; a music school in 1967, when Yehudi Menuhin gave a recital; and in 1970 a pyramidal exhibition hall designed by Sir Basil Spence. In 1967, separate new buildings originally planned as a girls' school were opened but changed to a junior boys' school the following year. Falling pupil numbers forced a change of use into an occasional conference centre until closure in 1980, and in 1987 it was redeveloped for the Commonwealth Agricultural Bureaux. Prince Charles came to perform the opening ceremony.

Fraser's house replaced a Georgian mansion known as Mongewell House sited on the other side of the stream flowing from the lake, where the headmaster's house now stands. A lease of 1865 shows it had 14 bedrooms and at least 16 other rooms [4]. In 1873 the mansion was described as 'large, extensive and of a domestic character . . . . a spacious lawn in front, with beautiful evergreens and a brook spanned by an ornamental Chinese bridge' [5]. Fraser bought the house in 1888 from the trustees of Dame Mary Anne Price [6], great niece of the Hon. Shute Barrington,

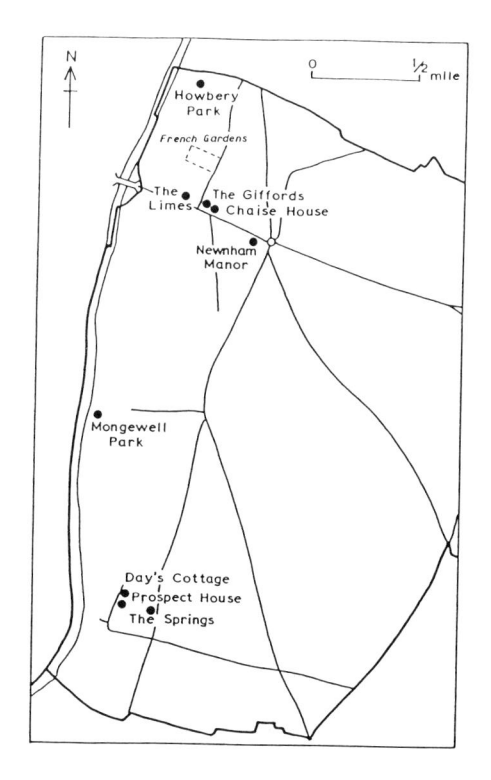

Positions of houses described.

bishop of Durham, who had the estate from 1770 until his death in 1826 [7]. Barrington acquired it through his second marriage, to Jane the only daughter and heiress of the previous owner, Sir John Guise of Rendcombe, Gloucestershire [8]. Their only son died as an infant in 1777. Barrington made great improvements over the years, landscaping the park and probably building the Georgian extension between 1770 and 1773, when he first began to stay there regularly as his favourite country residence. In 1775 it was referred to as 'the great house' [9]. The older part of the house was presumably the one listed as having 12 hearths in 1665, and described in the 1670 inventory of a former owner, Thomas Saunders, as having at least 10 rooms, with eight chambers as well as garrets. Saunders probably acquired the house following the death in 1649 of the previous owner, William Molins. The house then descended through Thomas's granddaughter Jane, who married Sir John Guise. Her mother, Anne Saunders, is commemorated by a tablet in Mongewell church.

Mongewell House, about 1876.

Shute Barrington was successively bishop of Llandaff (1769), Salisbury (1782) and Durham (1791). He a was scholar and a vigorous champion of the protestant establishment, yet friend of many dissenters and Roman Catholics. Not only was he active in helping parish clergy and the poor, but he was also much concerned with the welfare of Mongewell villagers, founding a shop on co-operative lines, and providing a trust fund for the maintenance of a free school (page 85) [10]. On occasions when he

The Hon. Shute Barrington, 1734-1826. Painted by Sir Thomas Lawrence, 1816. (Reproduced by courtesy of the Lord Bishop of Durham and the Church Commissioners for England; photograph: Courtauld Institute of Art.)

entertained a greater than usual company at the house, the villagers 'wonderingly and admiringly drew near to the windows . . . . and he was pleased to see them and he should certainly not interfere with their curiosity' [5]. At his death, among other positions that he held were the presidencies of the Society for Bettering the Condition of the Poor, and of the School for the Indigent Blind. In his will he gave numerous legacies to charities [8]. He was buried, as he wished, in Mongewell church. In the meadow to the north of his mansion house there used to be a fine avenue of elms. All that is left there now are the remains of a square stone monument which Barrington erected in 1800 with an inscription to the memory of two friends with whom he used to walk and talk beneath the trees [5].

**Howbery Park**

Prominent among the modern buildings of Hydraulics Research Limited, in Benson Lane, is an Elizabethan-style mansion of red brick and stone known as Howbery Park. It was started by William S. Blackstone after he bought the estate in 1833 [1]. Building work was slow, for it was still under way at the time of the 1851 census. There was then a carpenter, William Wakefield, living nearby with his family. Seven of his children had been born in Wallingford but his youngest son, then a three-year old, is listed as having been born in Crowmarsh, and he was named Howbery Wakefield! Perhaps this reflected his father's pleasure at getting such a long-term building job.

Although the mansion remained unfinished when Blackstone withdrew from public life, having been MP for Wallingford over some 20 years, his sister Jane lived there until 1858, when the estate was sold to Alfred and Edward de Mornay [12]. These two brothers finished the house to the original design, and then sold it in 1867 to Henry Bertie Watkin-Williams-Wynn [13], founder of Wallingford Cottage Hospital and a prominent member of the Primrose League, which was formed in 1884 by Lord Randolph Churchill to bring women into the work of the Conservative Party. It seems that Henry introduced the name Howbery Park, for earlier it had been called Howbery House. After he died, the house stayed empty until 1902, when it was bought by Harvey du Cros, later managing-director of the Dunlop Rubber Company [14]. In 1904 he drove to the top of Snowdon - a feat that would be frowned upon today! In 1909 an area of five acres near Howbery Farm was enclosed by du Cros for intensive market gardening under glass [15]. It was called French Gardens because the system had been developed in France, to satisfy demand for out-of-season fruit and vegetables. A nursery continued here until 1970. After lying derelict, with rejection of plans for house building in 1962 and 1974, the site was used by the South Oxfordshire District Council for its offices, opened in 1981. Harvey du Cros died in 1918 and Howbery Park was bought by Lord Wittenham of Rush Court, but after his death in 1931 the house remained unoccupied until 1940, when it was requisitioned by the Royal Engineers. After being used as an American military camp, a repatriation centre for prisoners-of-war, and then a Polish refugee camp, the

Howbery House, early 20th century .

estate was bought in 1950 by the Ministry of Works, and the Hydraulics Research Station was set up. In 1972 the buildings of the Institute of Hydrology were opened.

At the time of the sale in 1833 part of the estate was described as a 'site of a late mansion called Howbery Place', although all earlier references are to Howbery House. It had been built about 1755 by Robert Nedham after he had acquired Howbery manor. A poll of freeholders at the election of 1754 shows Bampton as his abode, so perhaps his new house had not been finished by then. It certainly had been by 1757, for Jackson's Oxford Journal records that on the morning of Thursday 10 February 'between 2 and 3 o'clock a most dreadful fire happened at Howbery . . . . which, not withstanding the greatest assistance, almost entirely destroyed the said house and all the furniture of value'. However, by 1759 two or three rooms were still being used. Robert died in 1762 and was buried in Crowmarsh. By 1766 the house had presumably been rebuilt because his widow, Catherine, was writing from there to her brother William Pitt (the elder, later earl of Chatham and prime minister) [16]. Both she and her son William lived intermittently at Howbery House [17]. In 1779 it was burgled, perhaps because it was left empty, and in 1789 it was up to let. Thereafter no reference has been found for several decades, but when William died in 1806 the estate passed to a distant cousin, the Rt. Hon. Francis Nedham, later earl of Kilmorey, who in his will of 1828 charged his trustees to sell or auction the house.

### Newnham Manor

The older part of this house was on the eastern side of the former Reading road that was realigned in 1862: it is shown there on the tithe map of 1847 and on a sketch map of 1803. Thomas Toovey lived there from 1778 to 1814. He had prospered, for in 1797 he bought Newnham Farm and other properties, so greatly enlarging his estate [18]. His son William Toovey lived there until his death in 1848, but by the next year Charles Hedges had the house. He was a member of the family firm of solicitors in Wallingford and brother of John Kirby Hedges, author of 'History of Wallingford'. In 1838 he had married William Toovey's daughter Ann, and he bought the estate from her brother and sister in 1855 [19]. The house is not mentioned in the 1851 census, so it was probably being enlarged at that time. It was known as Newnham House by 1841 and that name continued until about 1910, when major George Walsh acquired it and gave it its present name. During the Second World War the house was used as a school for deaf children.

## The Springs

This large, timber-framed, multi-gabled mansion, overlooking the lake at North Stoke, and now a hotel, was originally the home of Sir Alexander Condie Stephen, diplomat. It was built by 1897 on land belonging to the mill that he had bought in 1895 from St John's College, Oxford [20]. Sir Alexander provided a village cricket pitch on his land and arranged matches with local teams. He sold the house in 1902 to John Wormald, engineer, later managing-director of Mather & Platt Limited [21]. After extending the house in 1914, Wormald left The Springs in 1929 [22], having been knighted in 1919. He, too, was a local benefactor; for example he started the village school library in 1913. He also connected the village hall to his electric generator at the mill in 1923.

## The Limes

The small group of modern houses just east of Crowmarsh Gifford churchyard, known as The Limes, was built in 1976 on the site of a three-storey house of that name, occupied for about 50 years by Frank Wilder until his death in 1969. During the 1780s the house belonged to the Misses Knight [23], relatives of Robert Selwood, rector until 1749, so it may well have been his at one time. In 1789 it was sold to Thomas Willsden, but 20 years later it passed to Charles Allnatt [24]. In the late 19th century the house was improved by its architect occupier, Samuel Johns, who introduced its name.

### The Giffords

The Giffords was known early in the 19th century as Wicks [25], because Thomas Wicks had acquired the leasehold (for £29!) in 1791 [26], but the house may have been improved by mid-century when it was the home for five years of John Bradford, printer of Wallingford. The name The Giffords was used by Miss Florence Brown who lived there for 40 years from 1928.

### Chaise House

This 18th century house of silver grey bricks belonged in the middle of that century to the Creswells, farmers of Newnham Murren, but in 1853 it came into the hands of Sarah Owen [27], who lived there with her sister Mary until her death in 1881, and Mary continued until she too died, in 1892, leaving a £500 charity for the benefit of poor in the parish. In fact, both sisters had already been tenants of the house from about 1840 to 1850, so Mary had lived there for about 50 years. By the end of the century the house was called Roselea, and it was not until the late 1930s that Major Danby introduced the name Chaise House, presumably because the adjacent building had been used since the mid 19th century to house the chaise, or open carriage, used by the Misses Owen.

## Day's Cottage

Day's Cottage is so called because it was built by Anthony Day about 1795 on a plot just north of his farm house (now Prospect House) that he had sold in that year [28]. For over a century it was used as a shop, run firstly by three generations of the Higgs family, who were carpenters. James, and then his son William, had a grocery and beershop from about 1845. William's widow, Martha, bought the house from the widow of a servant of John Wilder, a baker of Ipsden, who himself had bought it in 1826 from Anthony Day's brother, Thomas.

## Prospect House

This 17th and 18th century house, with its cartwheel window over the front door, was at one time the home of Dame Clara Butt (1873-1936), world-famous contralto. She and her husband, Robert Kennerley-Rumford, are both buried in North Stoke churchyard. The earlier history of this house is less certain, but it seems to have been the home of Francis Reeves, carpenter, who in 1698 was bound over at Quarter Sessions to answer the accusation of his mother that she had been threatened and assaulted by her son and his wife. In the following year, the house passed to Robert Hill, shoemaker; and he in turn sold it in 1747 to Anthony Day, who seems to have developed it into a farmhouse [28]. In 1757 he was indicted, as parish constable, for not sending his yearly report to Quarter Sessions. After his death in 1788, his son, Anthony, sold the farm in 1795 to John Bennett of Dorrell's Farm (now Brook House), so the lands may then have been combined.

# 5. Roads

A medieval traveller, entering Crowmarsh after crossing Wallingford bridge, would have found the meeting of three highways. Ahead lay Crowmarsh Street, leading to Henley Way; to the right, Tidgeon Way went to Goring and beyond [1]; and to the left was a spur of the Icknield Way, that already ancient trackway from East Anglia to southern England, crossing the Thames at Goring [2]. It would have been a busy time on the Henley Way when the king came from London to Wallingford with all his followers. But its importance declined after 1416, when Abingdon bridge was built and took much of the traffic between London, Gloucester and South Wales [3].

For centuries to come, main roads were often in a poor state: the damage done by increasing traffic was beyond the repair resources of parishes. In 1386, the king ordered '. . . . all men of towns whatsoever lying around Wallingford who have wains . . . . one day in Easter week and one day in Whitsun week next . . . . to be ready with their wains upon warning . . . . to aid in leading to Crowmarsh stone and other things needful for repair of a certain way there which is rotten and dangerous . . . . whereby grievous hurt and peril has often happened to men, horses and wains . . . . and worse is like to happen if it be not repaired . . . .' [4]. From 1555, parishes had been made responsible for their sections; but there were other resources, for in the following year John Stamp of Newnham Murren bequeathed 3s 4d to 'Crowmarsh

# Roads

highway' and the year after that Richard Bristow, rector of Crowmarsh Gifford, similarly bequeathed 12d. In 1736, the inhabitants of Crowmarsh Gifford were indicted at Oxford Quarter Sessions for not maintaining the highway all the way from Wallingford bridge to Icknield Way.

From the 17th century, renewed efforts were made to keep roads in good order through the setting up of Turnpike Trusts. In 1765, certain gentlemen living in and near Crowmarsh acquired the power to turnpike the highway from Wallingford to Nuffield, where it met the already turnpiked highway from Dorchester and Benson to Henley [5]. There were no gates or tolls in Crowmarsh.

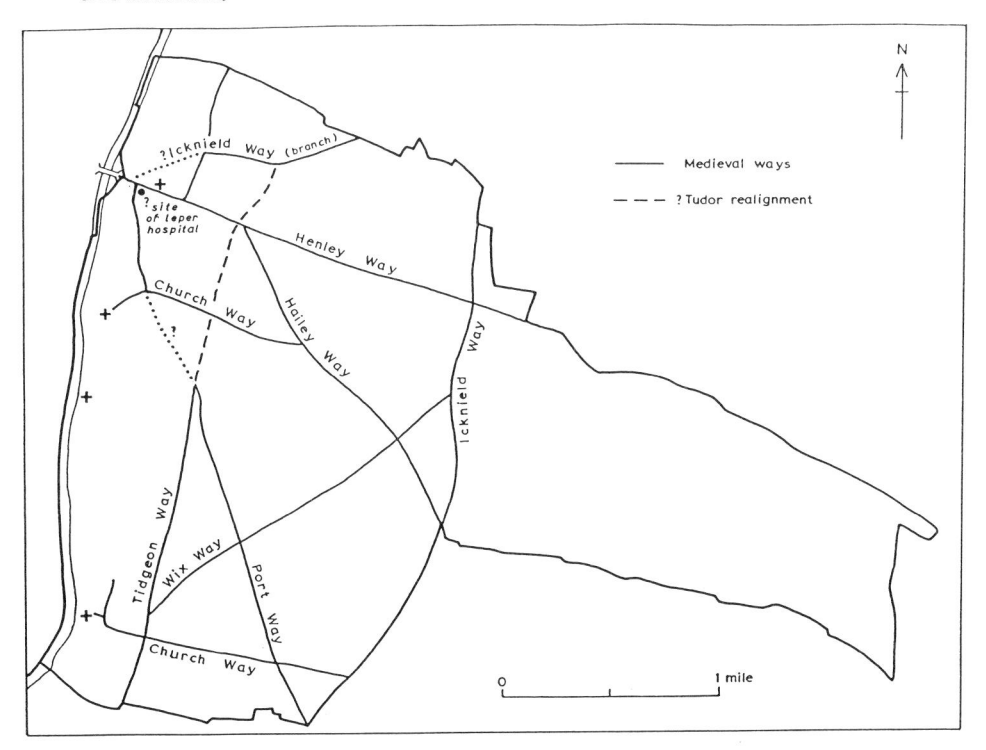

Former tracks and roads, and the probable site of the leper hospital.

Turnpike Trusts gradually became redundant, the Wallingford to Nuffield Trust probably about the mid 19th century for in 1855 the road was being referred to as 'formerly called London turnpike' [6]. In the meantime, the road had been realigned in the late 1820s from where it crossed the Icknield Way to the bottom of Gangsdown Hill, a change no doubt made necessary to avoid the worst parts of Brixton Hill [7].

Gravel for repairing the Street was carted from Blenheim pit [8], but the early 20th century saw the start of summer tarcoating by the County Surveyor to keep down the dust [9].

Tidgeon Way struck off southwards [10]. It almost certainly followed the line of modern Watery Lane to its junction with Church Way. The name appears in records from the 13th and 14th centuries [11] but subsequently only in reference to North Stoke, where it was clearly the modern Goring Road [12]. The link between Watery Lane and Goring Road was presumably the existing right-of-way across the fields to Grim's Ditch at Icehouse Hill. Such a route would have been more sensible than a more direct one southwards from Wallingford bridge, for it would have avoided the wet ground below the springs at Mongewell and North Stoke. Why was this route abandoned? Were there road improvements? The Old Reading Road, as it approaches Grim's Ditch from the north is bordered by hedges about five centuries old, judged by the shrub composition. This suggests a new road laid out in Tudor times, and the same is true for Clack's Lane and Lane End, which meets Crowmarsh Street at a former cross-roads, where the Reading Way used to start before its realignment in 1862 to start opposite the Bell [13]. That Clack's Lane did not exist in 1303 is suggested by a deed of that year which refers to 'the way leading to Swyncombe' that can only be Muddy (Marsh) Lane judged by the pieces of land mentioned [14].

The first known reference to Reading Way comes from the late 17th century [15], by which time Tidgeon Way had come to be known as Bacon Lane and it was only a bridle way [13]. Who was Bacon? In the early 13th century, a Walter Bacon had married the widow of Richard Morin, one time lord of Newnham manor and buried at Reading Abbey [10]. Moreover, Bacon's Close was the name of a meadow that now forms the southern part of the Bridge Villa camp-site, next to Watery Lane [16]. So it seems as though Tidgeon Way deteriorated to a bridle way, which it still is today; and no doubt its present name Watery Lane, used since the late 18th century, hints at former difficulties [17]. In 1688, for example, the inhabitants of Newnham were charged for not repairing Bacon Lane, and again in 1731 [13]. Watery Lane was enclosed by tall elm trees, and its appearance was much altered in the 1970s with the felling of those trees which had succumbed to Dutch elm disease. The Reading Way between the Street and Church Way was realigned in 1862 supposedly to shorten the distance to or from Wallingford and because it was 'very dark at night and generally wet and dirty'.

At Icehouse Hill another ancient route struck off southeastwards across the hills to Caversham, known from at least the 13th century as Port Way, a term often describing roads used to carry goods to market towns [18].

The Icknield Way runs from north to south on the east side of Ewelme, then crosses Crowmarsh along the present road past Blenheim and Forest Row, and continues as the footpath in Drunken Bottom (from Drincan, the Saxon name for the stream) into Ipsden parish. It has been known sometimes as Ickleton Way or Hackney Way. In North Stoke it seems to have been called Ewelme Way in the 17th and 18th centuries [12,19]. A spur went to Wallingford bridge, most likely continuing along the line of Muddy, or Marsh Lane (known as Swyncombe Way in 1303) where Clack's

Lane makes a right-angle bend, then along the right-of-way that passed through Howbery Park but was realigned in 1890, finally reaching the bridge by a way that existed in 1763 but has since gone out of use [20]. In the 17th century, Clack's Lane was known as Oxford Way, but in the next two centuries it became Shepherd's Lane or Watlington Way [15,21], and by the end of the 19th century it was known as both Broom's Lane and Clack's Lane.  Meanwhile, Muddy Lane was being called Steer's Lane by the 17th century [21,22]. Cox's (or Cox) Lane, formerly Hailey Lane, was presumably named after Thomas Cox, blacksmith, who lived for half of the 19th century on the corner where Chiltern Villa now stands.

Another short highway, Wix (Wicks) Way, ran from Tidgeon Way at the lake in North Stoke northeastwards across Port Way to the Icknield Way near where it crossed Henley Way [12,19].  It is mentioned from the 16th to 18th centuries. The western part still exists as a right-of-way, but the rest was closed in 1803 [13].

The present Benson Lane was known as Stockbridge Lane in the 17th century [22] and Shearman's Lane in the 18th [23]. It was probably used mainly for access to the fields, but had become a highway to Benson by 1783 [24].  Traffic this way was boosted in 1942 with the opening of the new road built to by-pass Benson airfield, which had been extended across the Oxford to Henley road.  Further increases led to demands from Crowmarsh for its own by-pass, and by 1960 a route was approved involving a roundabout behind the Bell and a new road north of the Street to Crowmarsh Hill, with a link through the Bell car park to the Old Reading Road [9].  But there were objections and a decision was delayed on the grounds of needing to wait for a decision on the route of the M4 [25].  In 1976, new by-pass plans were shown at a public exhibition, but the road was not finished until 1987.  The traffic lights which had been installed in 1967 at the busy junction of Benson Lane and the Street were then removed [26].

# 6. The Church

Of the early church in Crowmarsh, in the sense of a community of Christians, almost nothing is known. Individual parishioners willed small sums of money to parsons or to church buildings, but we know nothing of religious fervour or of conformity. Presumably the Reformation, of the early 16th century, was as dramatic as elsewhere, with a change to the new Protestant faith, but an element of Catholicism lingered to the end of the 18th century. Such 'papists' were to be found not only among the wealthier families, such as the Hildesleys of Howbery, but also among the less well off. We hear of Christopher Comber and his wife Joan in 1642, of widow Clack in 1685 (presumably Elizabeth, widow of Ralph Clack), and of Ann Smith a poor widow in 1700, all of them parishioners of Crowmarsh Gifford [1].

Non-conformity was represented in 1685 by Thomas North and his wife, Anabaptists. By the mid 18th century the Presbyterian Clare family had come to Newnham Murren, and by the early 19th century there were a few dissenting families in all four parishes, attending meetings in Wallingford [2]. In 1809, John Clare, by then a member of the Baptist church, and others unsuccessfully petitioned the bishop of Oxford to use John's house as a place of worship [3]. By the mid 19th century there were many dissenters, and John Trollope, rector of Crowmarsh Gifford, recorded in 1857 that 'there are many who never go anywhere', and that 'the limited means of the labouring clergy impede the welfare of the church' [4].

So, how well endowed were the clergy? All four parishes provided only small livings, even from combined tithes, glebe and offerings. Whereas many parsons seemed more or less content with their lot, some had more than one parish and could therefore live elsewhere, employing curates to minister to the parishioners, especially in the late 18th and early 19th centuries. During that period, curates' yearly stipends increased from about £15 to £60 for each parish. As for individual parsons and parsonage houses, there are considerable records.

All four parishes in Saxon times probably had their own rectors, but since then each parish has had a different history. Rectors continued at Mongewell up to this century, but in Crowmarsh Gifford and North Stoke rectors were replaced by vicars when the churches were granted to religious houses: Crowmarsh Gifford to Goring Priory by Walter of Bolbec (as recorded in a confirmatory charter of about 1181) [5], and North Stoke to Bromhall Priory (Windsor Park) by Richard II in 1391 [6]. Vicars continued to serve North Stoke after the church passed to St John's College, Cambridge, following the suppression of Bromhall Priory in 1521 [7], whereas in Crowmarsh Gifford the appropriation of the church to Goring Priory seems to have been annulled about 1480, when rectors returned to the parish. However, a yearly pension of 10s was still being paid to the Priory in 1535 out of rents from land in Crowmarsh, as well as £3 from the parson [8]. All this time, Newnham Murren, like Ipsden, had been a chapelry attached to North Stoke, as witnessed by the 1291 tax returns of Pope Nicholas.

The parsons, whether rectors or vicars, had very modest incomes from their small parishes. In 1425, for example, following complaint by parishioners of North Stoke to the archbishop that the vicar had not sufficient maintenance, Bromhall Priory was ordered to pay him 10½ marks (£7) a year [9].

Although the names of most parsons have been recorded in the bishops' registers since medieval times, it is not until the 16th century that much more is known about them. However, in North Stoke two of the medieval rectors have memorials in the church: Robert of Estall (1238-1275) and Roger Parker (1340-1356). The marble slab of Robert of Estall has the remains of a marginal inscription of inlaid brass letters, the 'M' having the unusual shape associated with brasses made in Lincolnshire. Before the formation of the diocese of Oxford in 1542, all four parishes were in the diocese of Lincoln. Thomas Bradshaw (vicar 1523-1554) survived the assault made on him in 1525 (see p. 128) and in 1548 he covenanted with St John's College to build a new vicar's mansion on an adjacent plot of land [10]. Stephen Cardinal (1571-1576), in his will made only three days before he was buried at Ipsden, ensured upkeep of the new house by charging his successor 'to bind himself to my executor and two of the substantial men of this parish to leave it in as good estate unto his successor as he found it'. Edmund Cass (1611-1630), in a letter to the College dated 22 March 1612 (and received 27 July!) requested help because of his poor means and the voluntary support he was providing for the the previous incumbent's mother. He was granted £13 6s 8d [11]. His probate inventory of 1630 shows the vicarage house had three rooms downstairs with five chambers over, and among his possessions were books, a sword and a musket with bandoleers. Samuel Peachie (1648-1663) ordered in his will that he should 'be buried without any sermon or conflux of people'. In 1683, Thomas Longland (1663-1698) was requested by the College bursar to provide information on parish income, and in his reply he explained that 'an earnest inquiry into such things will but awaken suspicion and great jealousies . . . . in those who can give me due information . . . . and they [are] ever shy and cautious of ever discoursing with me of such concerns' [12]. Two years later, his son William was touched by James II for the 'king's evil', in the hope of a cure for scrofula - neck swellings due to tuberculous

Church Cottages, North Stoke.

glands [13]. Richard Headlam (1698-1730), with the College, petitioned the bishop of Oxford for permission to build a new vicarage house at Ipsden. It was completed in 1701, and thereafter the former vicarage house was let for rent. It still stands today as two church cottages. He bequeathed £100 for the interest to be used to provide coats for poor men of Ipsden, and the charity became combined with William Emery's (see page 111). William Thomas (1736-1767) added a further five acres of land for the Emery charity.

Of the rectors of Mongewell, Simon Astley (1518-1556) seems to have had a comfortable existence, for his will mentions three servants. By contrast, the inventory of Francis Hodson's goods, drawn up in 1671, amounted to only just over £13, of which £5 13s 4d were for study books. He also had a brown nag valued at £3. We can picture this studious man of slender means riding out to visit parishioners. He seems to have lived not in a rectory but in Mongewell House, judged by a reference to the 'parsonage room' in the

1670 probate inventory of Thomas Saunders, lately lord of the manor. Moreover, a glebe terrier of 1485 makes no mention of a parsonage house [14]. When such a house was first built is not known: perhaps it was during the incumbency of Robert Selwood, a gentleman from Abingdon who, after being rector for 47 years, in 1749 bequeathed £1,000 to each of his two granddaughters as well as smaller sums to his two servants. Robert Price (who became rector in 1776 through the patronage of his uncle Shute Barrington, owner of the Mongewell estate and by then bishop of Llandaff) greatly improved the house around 1780 [15]. In 1805 it was described as being of brick with a stable, garden and orchard amounting to about one acre. There were also five acres of glebe land that had been given by the bishop [16]. Price became a canon of Salisbury in 1785, and by 1790 he spent most of his time there. Next year he resigned as rector and David Durell, a Jersey man, was instituted, staying for 60 years. But he, too, was absent part of each year as prebend of Durham from 1801. In 1813 he replied to the bishop of Oxford that it was no longer than three months in a year, and similarly in 1827 [17]. In 1838 he was no longer capable of performing any part of his duties, and by 1843 he had become afflicted by rheumatism. Before then he had been active in community life becoming, for example, a trustee of the Oxford Provident Bank in 1818, and joining the clergy who were outstanding in their weekly attendance at board meetings of the Radcliffe Infirmary [18]. The last rector of Mongewell was Thomas Hughes (1893-1927), who finished his incumbency under a shadow due to an alleged scandal that prompted the lord of the manor, Alexander Fraser, to forbid his employees from attending church services. After Hughes died the rectory was pulled down.

In Crowmarsh Gifford, Richard Bristow (1550-1557) came from a yeoman family that lived for several generations at North Stoke Farm, and by his will gave two candlesticks to the church (were they to replace the ones removed by commissioners appointed by

Henry VIII under the Chantry Act of 1545?) [19], as well as money to poor households in Crowmarsh and 'Newnamsyde'. Perhaps the latter referred to the Newnham side of Crowmarsh Street. Several later rectors served the parish for long spells: Evan Roberts (1577-1615), Edmund Trulock (1615-1671) and Robert Selwood (1690-1750). It may have been Trulock who rebuilt the parsonage, for in a 1644 description of the church there is mention of a new brick house [20]. It seems not to have been a substantial place because in 1665 he paid tax on only one hearth. This is consistent with a description of the parsonage house in 1677, when it was said to be in two parts: one next to the churchyard on the south side and in good repair, the other separate to the north and decayed. In that year the rector, William King, requested permission of the bishop to pull down the older building and add to the newer one a 27-foot building with a cellar to make the house 'large enough for an ordinary family' [21]. His request seems to have been granted for by 1680 the rectory was described as a dwelling house with outhouses and a garden [22], the latter no doubt including an adjoining strip of the churchyard that King was allowed to take. After the death of Robert Selwood, for nearly another hundred years only curates lived there. For example, in 1759 the then rector, James Lea, wrote to the bishop: 'I do not reside upon my living, it being a small one. Your lordship's predecessor was so kind as to dispense with my non-residence on that consideration and my having a large family. I have a licenced curate residing in the parsonage house. His salary is £24 p.a. and surplice fees' [23]. David Durell (1792-1844), a year after he became rector (while also rector of Mongewell), had trees from the churchyard cut down to repair his house. By early in the 19th century even the curates were living in Benson or Wallingford, and in 1838 the house was described by Durell as 'a very inferior residence' [24]. By then the curate had a yearly stipend of £150, but his duties included Newnham Murren. John Trollope (1844-1878), third cousin of Anthony Trollope the novelist, much improved the house in 1845, after coming from South Stoke to be rector of Crowmarsh Gifford. Further changes to the parsonage house were made early this century, but in 1979 it was sold as a private residence.

The main source of a parson's income was tithe: originally a tenth part of the produce of a parish, the crops being stored in a tithe barn on the glebe (land owned by the parson for his benefit). In Crowmarsh Gifford, the remains of the tithe barn, at the corner of Lane End according to the tithe map, were pulled down in 1987. It was known as the tithe barn in the mid 19th century, but not by 1900, presumably because tithes in kind had been commuted to cash payments in 1845. A glebe terrier of 1685 describes it as 'a large barn containing five bays . . . . with backside belonging' [25]; and in 1662 the inventory of the goods of William Sadler, drawn up following his death, lists 20 quarters of peas and barley in the 'parsonage barn'. In Mongewell the tithe barn used to be in the rectory garden but when Robert Price became rector the lord of the manor, Shute Barrington, had it moved in 1772 to newly-exchanged glebe in Mill Close, on the south side of the lake. Subsequently, David Durell assigned the barn to the bishop in return for further glebe, making five acres in all [26]. After that there is no further mention of the tithe barn, neither in the glebe terrier of 1805 nor on the tithe map of 1840. In North Stoke, a parsonage barn existed in 1662, for Robert Dorrell's inventory of that year shows he had 40 quarters of wheat and rye there, as well as 24 quarters of barley. Presumably the barn was on the ancient rectorial glebe, and is therefore likely to be the barn still standing in the grounds of present-day Rectory Farm House. In addition to tithes, the vicar of North Stoke had 20 acres of glebe, listed in terriers of 1685, 1762 and 1808 [27], whereas the rector of Crowmarsh Gifford had no glebe, although there were two acres of land the rents of which went to repairing the church.

# The Church

Crowmarsh civil parish comprises much of the area of the four ancient ecclesiastical parishes of Crowmarsh Gifford, Newnham Murren, Mongewell and North Stoke. These were themselves presumably created when England was divided into parishes in the 7th century. Their boundaries are likely to have been set by those of the Saxon estates (page 8). The upper parts of Newnham Murren and Mongewell were incorporated into Stoke Row in 1849 [28].

Presumably there were Saxon churches in all four parishes, but almost nothing of them seems to have survived. The existing buildings are all of Norman origin. Those at Newnham Murren and North Stoke (along with Ipsden) were built in the 12th century by monks from Bec Abbey (near Brionne), where accounts for 1288 show that tithes from Newnham and North Stoke were among its revenues [29]. Both churches are dedicated to St Mary, the patroness of Bec.

The **church of St Mary Magdalene**, Crowmarsh Gifford, comprises chancel and nave from at least the time of king Stephen (early 12th century), when it was apparently used as a fortified post in his war against Matilda (page 132)[30]. A small north transept was added about 1200. The Norman west doorway has an arch of three orders, and above it are two small circular openings and a central arched window, the whole popularly known as 'eyes, nose and mouth'. About 1840, a restoration by William S. Blackstone unblocked the west doorway but sealed up the Norman south doorway, which had been depicted with a porch in 1822 [31]. Inside, the high and wide chancel arch is original, as also is the fine piscina with an arched opening and projecting fluted bowl, probably one of the oldest in England [32]. The Norman font has an arcade of spiral-fluted columns. The windows have jumbled pieces of Belgian stained glass, some dating from the 16th and 17th centuries [33]. About 1880, the west door, with supposed bullet holes from the Civil War, was moved to the entrance of the vestry, on the north side of the church.

The Church 73

Crowmarsh Gifford church about 1880. The elms were felled in 1882.

Interior of Crowmarsh Gifford church after the restoration of 1894.

It has been claimed that the church was once the chapel of the medieval leper hospital (page 104), but the available evidence is against that idea. Not only are the names of known hospital chaplains quite different from those of the parish priests at the time, but also the chapel was sold by the Crown after the dissolution of the monasteries [34].

The **church of St Mary,** Newnham Murren, comprises chancel with original north and south windows, nave with original north doorway, and a south aisle with an arcade of two arches and an octagonal pier [32]. On the south side of the chancel arch is a small circular squint, or hagioscope. In 1849 the building was much restored, at a cost of £500. Since at least the 13th century this church had been a chapel attached to the mother church of St Mary, North Stoke, but in 1908 it was joined with Crowmarsh Gifford [35]. It went out of regular use after the First World War, and was closed in 1961 when a fault in the chancel arch made the building unsafe [36]. It was rescued from dereliction in the 1960s by Hugh Vaux before being taken over by the Redundant Churches Fund in 1975 [37].

Originally a small building, the **church of St John the Baptist,** Mongewell, was restored and extended by Shute Barrington in 1791, when the battlemented polygonal bell turret was built [38]. A further restoration of 1881 added the dog-tooth decoration on the chancel arch [39]. In 1923 the benefice was united with North Stoke, but following the death of the last rector, in 1932, the church closed and it quickly fell into decay, though in 1954 the chancel was restored and reconsecrated [40]. Few services were held each year and the building was finally vested in the Redundant Churches Fund in 1985, with the site to be maintained by Carmel College. In 1986 repairs were made to leave the remains of the church tidy and safe, and the chancel and tower still stand.

# The Church 75

West end, Crowmarsh Gifford church.

Newnham Murren church, early 19th century.

The **church of St Mary the Virgin,** North Stoke, comprises chancel and nave, rebuilt in the 13th and 14th centuries, respectively. The north door has ironwork of the 14th century and a 15th century wooden porch. Above the blocked south doorway is a unique mass dial, probably 14th century, with head and hands of a priest [41]. The lower part of the tower, of flint with stone dressings and angle buttresses, is of 14th century, but the upper part is dated 1725 on the west side and it relaces one that fell in the late 17th century. The bishop of Lincoln's visitation of 1530 records 'the chancel suffers deficiency in glass windows' [42]. Repairs were made to the chancel in 1772, after it had been described in 1765 as 'ruinous in the tyleing, being full of gutters or valleys, and is occasioned by the laths and sparrs being decayed' [43]. During a full restoration in 1902, 14th century wall paintings were discovered in the nave: over the chancel arch is the Last Judgement; to the left of the pulpit is the martyrdom of St Thomas Becket; on the side walls are narrative scenes, the martyrdoms of St Catherine and St Stephen on the north side, and the

North Stoke church. Heating was installed in 1915.

Fourteenth century mass dial, North Stoke church.

Passion on the south side; and on the window splays are saints and a red demon [44]. In the chancel are a few medieval tiles, and 16th century oak benches with ends having linen-fold carving. The lych-gate was given in 1925 by Dame Clara Butt and her husband, Captain Kennerley-Rumford, in memory of their son, Roy. The wood came from the old bridge over the Thames at Goring [45].

Successive acts of Parliament in the 16th and 17th centuries promoted the parish as an area for secular administration, gradually superseding the manorial court. Churchwardens were elected by the vestry and they had many duties. Meetings were sometimes held by the churchwardens for the parishioners to have their say. For example, one was held in Crowmarsh Gifford in 1861 when Alfred de Mornay attempted to stop up a footpath between Benson Lane and the church; the people successfully appealed. For many years in the 19th century Mongewell held its vestry meetings in the convivial surroundings of either the George Hotel at Wallingford or the Town Arms, before returning home in 1879 to use the schoolroom [46].

Under the Local Government Act of 1894 the civil functions of the vestries were transferred to new Parish Councils and Parish Meetings. Each rural parish was required to have a Parish Meeting at least once a year. Small parishes did not have to elect a Council if the Parish Meeting decided against it, and in fact only Crowmarsh Gifford chose to have a Council. Its first meeting was held on 4 December 1894 in the schoolroom (later Parish House); on the agenda were the village water supply and the allotments. James Guttridge, the local photographer, was the clerk, and duly recorded the occasion in the minute book which Councils and Meetings were obliged to keep. Because of their close proximity, on either side of the Street, Crowmarsh Gifford Parish Council and Newnham Murren Parish Meeting had to co-operate over matters ranging from street lighting to celebrations. When North Stoke wanted to effect an exchange of village green in 1896 it had to apply to the County Council to confer on the Parish Meeting the powers of a Parish Council for this purpose. Administration obviously became simpler when the four parishes were united to become one civil parish in 1932 [47].

Crowmarsh has several times resisted attempts to incorporate part of it into the borough of Wallingford [48].

# 7. School

Very few village children went to school before the 19th century. Most of their parents thought education was unnecessary, and anyway deprived them of the chance for children to work and supplement meagre family incomes. Evenso, in 1689, Robert Burgess of Wallingford, a graduate of St John's College, Oxford, was teaching boys in Crowmarsh Gifford and Newnham Murren [1]. In 1768, Catherine, wife of Robert Nedham of Howbery Park, paid for the instruction of 12 or 14 boys and girls from Crowmarsh Gifford [2]. By about 1795 a school for 20 to 30 children was being supported by subscriptions from well-wishers, but it is not known where. In 1808, reading and needlework were being taught. The same or a similar school is recorded well into the 19th century [3], but in 1844 William S. Blackstone, until that year the owner of Howbery, built a schoolroom on the west side of Benson Lane at a cost of £300 [4]. It was soon made available to the rector, John Trollope, newly arrived from South Stoke, where he had already established a village school. Trollope had insufficient funds to open the Crowmarsh school for in 1846 he describes it as 'merely the bare walls with a grate'. He was writing to the National Society, hoping for assistance with some fittings. The Society was a voluntary organisation that had been set up in 1811 to provide funds for schools 'promoting the education of the poor in the principles of the established church'. A sum of £3 16s 9d was estimated for an 8 feet long writing

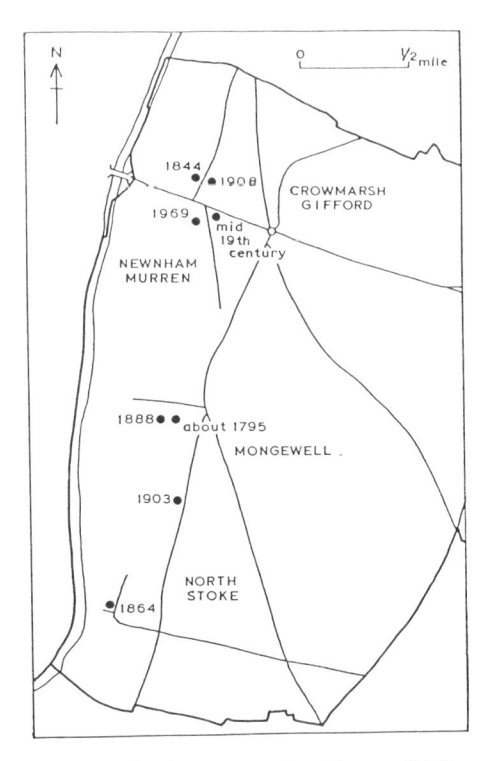

Schools founded over the last 200 years.

desk, two forms, and 22 feet of hat rail and wood pegs, but no grant was given. In 1850 the school was united with the National Society [5]. The room was sold to the rector in 1858 for £150, towards which the Society granted £20 [6]. For several decades the single teacher was the wife or widow of a local craftsman, whose income was thereby eked out by the children's fees of a few pence each week [7]. Such 'dame schools' probably provided a very limited education.

By 1871, 47 children were attending, and Martha, wife of George Belcher, a shoemaker, was the teacher. The room was 38 feet by 15 feet, adequate for the 10 square feet allowed for each child. In 1874, William Reynolds became the teacher, and the following year saw the start of the school log, from which we get much detailed information. Following the 1876

Education Act, which required full-time schooling for five to ten year olds, attendance increased and exceeded 70 by 1882. It is therefore not surprising that Her Majesty's Inspector reported in that year 'the accommodation for infants is no longer adequate, and if the number of infants attending the school continues as high as it now is I cannot recommend the payment of further grant for the infants until proper accommodation is provided for them'. In April 1885 a new room, 20 feet by 13 feet, was added at the rear.

For all these children there was one teacher, one pupil teacher and a monitor. In 1895, however, the managers thought it 'desirable in the interests of the school that a master and mistress should if possible be obtained' [8]. They gave Elizabeth Dust three months' notice, after ten years as mistress, and appointed John Burden, with his wife to take the needlework. But by 1898 he had agreed to resign because the managers were unable to afford both him, at £90 a year, and a pupil teacher at £40. They

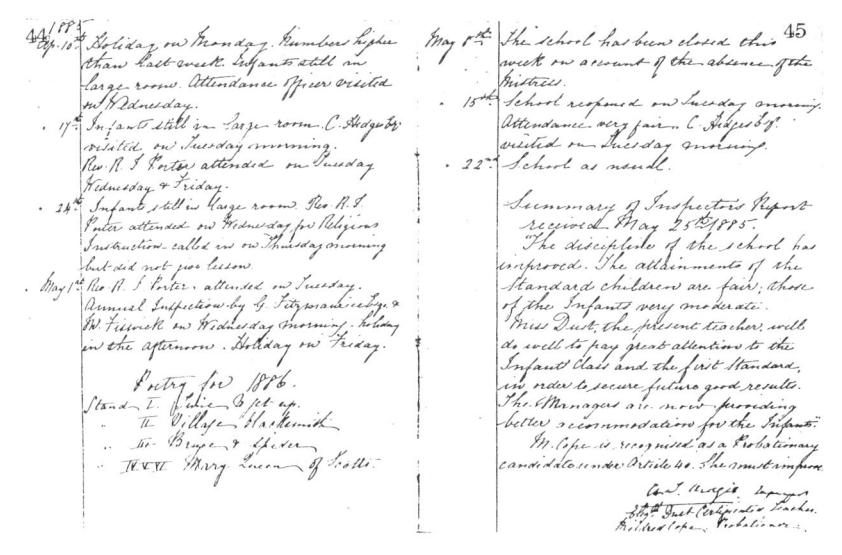

From Crowmarsh Gifford school log book for 1885, showing the inspector's report, bottom right.

(Courtesy of the Headmaster.)

82     School

1900: the teachers were William and Lillian Titler.

1928: the teachers were Mary Rathbone and Louisa Chapman.

thought it better to obtain a master whose sister or wife would be able to take the work of the pupil teacher, at a joint salary of £110 a year. So William Titler became teacher, with his wife as assistant, and the pupil teacher left. But not for long, because in 1900 Her Majesty's Inspector recommended more staff, and a pupil teacher returned.

Attendance continued at 60 to 80 around the turn of the century, when there were three teachers: the head, his wife and an infants' mistress. School lasted from 9 am to 4 pm, with 12 to 2 pm as midday break. At age eight, infants moved into the 'big school', as the main room was called, where six classes, or 'standards' were in the one room. Lessons were reading, writing, arithmetic, singing, reciting, drama, English grammar and general knowledge. William Titler flogged rather than caned his pupils, and in 1902 he resigned after protests from many parents [9].

By 1901, Her Majesty's Inspector reported 'the main room is sometimes overcrowded. When the school

Inside Crowmarsh Gifford school, about 1908.

was visited in June, 52 children were present, there being desk accommodation for only 45'. And in 1903, even the new infants' room was described as 'very small, and great difficulty therefore exists in providing for sufficient movement or exercise'. With such close packing it is not surprising that there were outbreaks of disease. In 1905, for example, the school was closed in June because 19 children were absent with measles.

By then the Board of Education was demanding a new school. If funds could not be found from voluntary subscriptions the County would have to find them out of the rates. In 1906, plans were drawn up for a new one-room infants' school for 32 children, and in the following year a joint Parish Meeting decided unanimously to build the school and to continue it as a Church of England school. The managers agreed in January 1908, but it would be a two-room mixed school for 68 children (still at 10 square feet a child) opposite the old school on a quarter-acre site sold by Frank Dore, owner of Coldharbour. By then, £750 had been collected from subscribers. The building was put up at a cost of £988, and opened on 17 September 1908 by the bishop of Oxford. Infants continued to use the old school, which had been converted to take 40 children. Within two months both schools had to close because there were six cases of diphtheria, five in one family.

Swimming lessons, at Lower Wharf, Wallingford, started in 1930, and provision of children's milk in 1934. By that year, numbers had fallen to only 24, and indeed the old school had been taken out of use in 1926 and subsequently leased to the British Legion, Crowmarsh and District Branch, as a club house. It came into use again, however, in January 1940, as numbers swelled suddenly to about 50 with the arrival of evacuees. One highlight was the start of hot dinners in 1945, prepared at Mongewell school.

After the Second World War, numbers increased and in 1953 the old school was brought into use again as an extra classroom. 70 children were on the roll. By 1955 it was also being used as a school canteen. Plans for extension were announced in 1956, but in 1959 a start on building was first delayed because of realignment of the proposed by-pass, and later abandoned in favour of a new school. Permission for one in Old Reading Road was given in 1960, but building had to be deferred in 1961 through lack of funds; instead, a temporary room was added in the following year [10]. With the population of Crowmarsh increasing by nearly a half during the 1960s, there were renewed demands for a new school. Work on it started in March 1968, and the opening was a year later. Accommodation was for 160, but an extension was added in 1972. Betty Hasthorpe, who taught at the school for 38 years before retiring in 1977, was in charge all through these difficult times.

A plan to convert the 1908 school into a village hall was abandoned because of high costs, and in 1973 it was sold for £10,400 [11]. As for the 1844 school, after use by local organisations it was named Parish House in 1980, but because it was not widely used it was sold and converted to a private residence, in 1984.

Newnham Murren children used Crowmarsh Gifford school, although from about 1815 the parish did have its own school, for about 30, supported by their pence and subscriptions. It is not known if this became the dame school between Home Farm and the Old Reading Road, where Sarah, widow of William King, a carpenter, was the teacher from about 1850 into the 1860s [12].

In Mongewell, a day school for about 10 children was established around 1795 by Shute Barrington [13]. It was a single room at the west end of one of the cottages he had built for his estate workers in 1780. The teacher in 1871 was Lizzie, wife of James Freeman, a tallowchandler of Wallingford. She had a monitress to help in her dame school. An infants' room was added in 1885, but the building was abandoned in 1888 in favour of a more spacious estate school built just to the west by the lord of the manor, Alexander Fraser [14]. The teacher's salary at this time was £60 a year - more than the 4s a week that it was in 1833! There was accommodation for 59 children, but the school did not last long, for a two-room council school was built in 1903 on the Goring Road just across the border in North Stoke parish. Attendance stayed at around 30 but swelled at the outbreak of the Second World War with evacuees from London. Numbers fell again after the war until the school was closed in 1971, and then converted in 1974 to a study centre for primary school children [15].

A day school for about ten children was established in North Stoke around 1805, supported by subscriptions, but its site is unknown [13]. In 1864, the vicar, Richard Twopeny, provided a new one-room school, with the assistance of St John's College, Cambridge, and the Dodds of North Stoke Farm. About 30 children attended and the teacher was Ann Wicks from Ipsden, who had taught at the previous school. Although illiterate, 'she had the art of teaching and enforcing discipline', so that 'the children of this school take precedence of other schools in the local examinations' [16]. After about 25 years she was followed by Charlotte, wife of John Goff, a shepherd. The school had closed by 1893, with the children going to the new Mongewell school [17], and the building became the Parish Room, but it was less used after the village hall was put up in 1911. Since 1971, primary school age children from both Mongewell and North Stoke have been bussed to Crowmarsh Gifford school.

# 8. Craftsmen and Shopkeepers

For centuries many of the everyday goods needed in the house and on the farm were made locally, often by village craftsmen. Apart from the all-important miller, there were workers in, for example, iron, wood, leather and cloth. Other goods came from afar and were sold in shops, but village shops were almost unknown before the 19th century. Crowmarsh reflected these trends, and sufficient records have survived to tell us who some of these craftsmen and shopkeepers were and what they did.

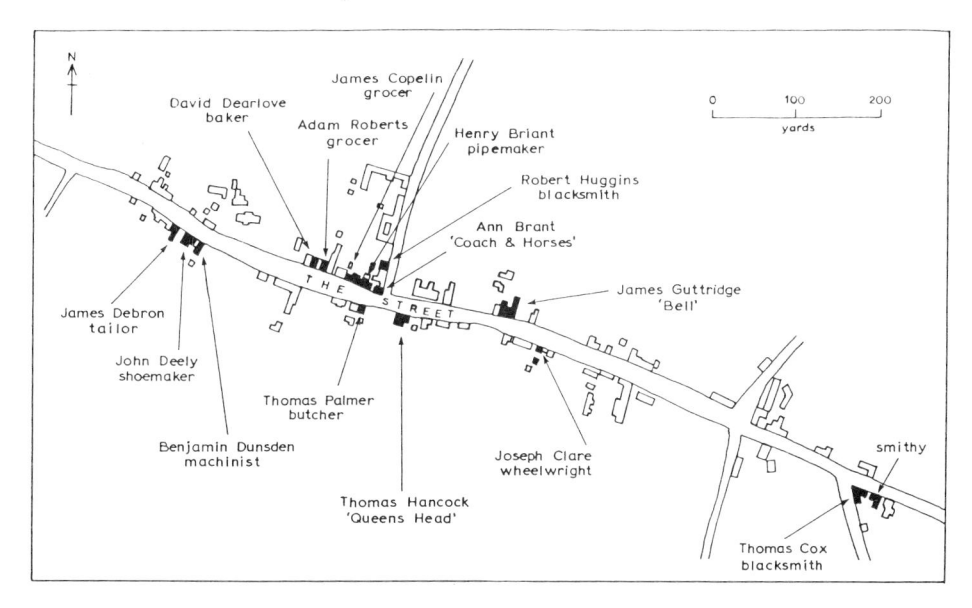

Craftsmen and shopkeepers in the 1840s.

## Craftsmen

Domesday Book records two mills at each of North Stoke, Mongewell and Crowmarsh, but we do not know where they stood. Presumably those in North Stoke and Mongewell were on the brooks flowing from the springs. One of those in Crowmarsh may have been in what is now part of Benson parish, but a water mill was certainly part of Crowmarsh manor in 1264, although there is no mention of it in 1287 [1]. Perhaps it stood on the low ground just upstream of Wallingford bridge. No mill is recorded as ever having been at Newnham.

In the early 16th century a mill at North Stoke seems to have gone with Rectory Farm, judged by the 1515 will of Katherine Bolter, who had leased the farm from Bromhall Priory in 1511 [2]. Almost nothing is known about such early millers as Richard Roberts (1555) and William Corderoy (1669), but from the early 18th century the Clarke family were millers for at least six generations, five of whom were named Joseph. The first married in 1716 Mary, daughter of Robert Dorrell of Burghfield, now Brook House. The second was described as a mealman in 1755 [3], when a datestone was fixed to the garden wall naming Joseph Clarke 'scener' and 'juner'. The fifth Joseph

North Stoke mill, about 1904. The cottages have gone.

mortgaged the mill in 1851, just before the death of his wife and only child, the mill subsequently going to his nephew Robert. No miller is known after 1891, so presumably the mill ground its last corn about then. By 1902 the millhouse was a private residence.

Mongewell mill was part of the manorial estate. When Edward Guilding took over the tenancy in 1819 the lease defined certain rights that probably had existed for a long time, including the 'liberty to convey corn, grain and flour in boats to and from the mill along the brook between the mill and the river Thames'. There was also a condition that the miller 'will from time to time grind and dress . . . . gratis all such grain and flour as the owners for the time being of Mongewell Manor House . . . . shall respectively continue to occupy the same' [4]. There is no record of a miller after the 1881 census, so presumably it stopped working soon after Alexander Fraser came to Mongewell House, in 1878.

Malt for brewing was often prepared at home, and individual farms had malthouses among their outbuildings. For example, the 1614 probate inventory of the goods of Thomas Clack of Crowmarsh Gifford shows his malthouse contained, among other things, a malt mill, a yeotting trough (for soaking barley) and two seedlips (containers for carrying seed at sowing). In the 18th century, community malthouses became more numerous. One stood in Crowmarsh Street where the houses now face Jewsons. It was mentioned in 1755, when the maltster was Edward Hutton the elder [3]. He had been born in Mongewell but was already a yeoman farmer in Crowmarsh Gifford by 1715 [5]. In 1755 he sold the malthouse to Joseph Clarke, miller of North Stoke, as the marriage portion of Joseph's sister Sarah, who was to marry Edward Hutton the younger. When Edward the younger died in 1772 (and was buried under the south side of the yew tree in Crowmarsh Gifford churchyard [6]), the malthouse passed to the five sons and daughters of his sister Elizabeth, who had married Richard Allnatt, a farmer from North Stoke who had come to Crowmarsh Gifford about 1740. These five insured it in 1774 against fire for £280 [7]. The policy describes the building as being constructed of brick, stone and timber, panelled with brick, and tiled. By 1790 the malthouse was owned by their cousin John Allnatt, an attorney of Wallingford. Around this time there was an exciseman living in Crowmarsh. He is last mentioned in 1795, so perhaps the malthouse went out of use about then. Certainly by 1826 it had been pulled down, and a row of seven small cottages was soon built on the site [3]. These were reached from the Street by a narrow passage that still exists and that came to be known later in the century as The Alley.

Apart from a few names, little is known of Crowmarsh blacksmiths until the mid 18th century, when John Dyer made his shop out of a barn or stable on the north side of the Street about halfway between Benson Lane and Clacks Lane [8]. He had moved across the road by 1759, the year in which he inherited a house there. The shop, however, seems not to have moved, even when John was succeded by Thomas Cox, about 1790. His son, another Thomas Cox, moved from Crowmarsh Gifford to Newnham Murren about 1830 and was at the corner of Cox's Lane (now Meadow Lane) by 1841, when he built a new smithy that still stands there. Thomas was helped by his brother-in-law, James Allnatt, who eventually took over the smithy and Thomas became a farrier and vet. When James died in 1863 his son Henry carried on until he retired at the end of the century, when the smithy became a stable. By then there was only a jobbing blacksmith - Henry Clark, at the Bell - and even he gave up his business in 1899 to Walter Wilder [9].

The iron foundry of Walter Wilder & Sons Ltd, on the site of the yard of old Howbery Farm, was started about 1868 by Leonard Wilder, who moved from Wallingford into the old farmhouse [10]. The works spread east to include old farm buildings, a few remains of which still stand. Following Leonard's death in 1887, his son Walter took over, and by 1911 the firm had acquired the name it is known by today.

Newnham Murren smithy, in use until about 1900.

They made castings, mainly for agricultural machinery but also for street lamps and drain covers. Following Walter, three sons continued the business: Walter, a craftsman in ornamental metal work who had a fine tenor voice; Percival; and Frank, whose son David continues as director.

Early in the 19th century, threshing machines came widely into use, to the great concern of farm workers, who feared for their jobs (see page 127). Nevertheless, some craftsmen turned their hands to making and repairing them, along with other farm machines. The first to set up business in Crowmarsh was Benjamin Dunsden, formerly a wheelwright who had come from Wallingford to Newnham Murren about 1810. By 1841 he was an engineer living in the easternmost house in Crowmarsh Gifford on the south side of the Street (see map on page 87). After his death in 1860, his son James Dunsden continued the business but turned to carpentry before retiring to live across the Street next to grocer Richard Smith. In the meantime, James Luker, living a few doors away, had become involved in the same work, perhaps with Benjamin, but during the 1860s he returned to being a farm worker as the need for village machinists declined.

## Craftsmen and Shopkeepers

The wheelwright's craft in Crowmarsh passed from father to son. When John Clare came in the 1750s he was the first of five generations of Clare wheelwrights there [11]. The land tax returns and tithe map show they lived at the house still standing west of Home Farm, with the workshop at the rear. After his death in 1839 his son Joseph carried on the business, followed by his grandson Charles, who moved across the Street to part of the yard of old Howbery Farm now occupied by Collier Bros. About 1870 Charles Bowden took over there, the start of another father-son succession. After his death his son Henry added coach building to his business, and by 1910 this had become his only craft, presumably because the demand for a wheelwright's work was declining. Evenso, Thomas Lovegrove, formerly of the Gardeners Arms, carried on in Newnham Murren until about 1930. As coach building declined in turn, Henry turned between the wars to painting motor car bodies. He is said to have put on seven coats after refurbishing the Rolls-Royce belonging to Howard Gould of Mongewell House.

The Clares' house today. Their workshop was at the rear.

Many Crowmarsh carpenters worked for only a few years or changed their craft, judged by entries in old trade directories, but the King family stayed for four generations - all named William! The first William King came in 1761, when he was married in Crowmarsh Gifford. By 1789 he had moved to Newnham Murren for in that year the churchwardens' account book records 5s 10½d paid to him for work done in the church. He probably lived at the same place as his son and grandson, whose widow, Sarah, a schoolmistress (page 85), was last heard of in 1861 at a house formerly near the corner of Old Reading Road [12].

There seem to have been more carpenters than wheelwrights for North Stoke had its own, at least until the mid 19th century.

For two centuries Crowmarsh nearly always had at least one shoemaker or bootmaker, until Les Foster retired in 1983. We know their names and where they lived, but little else. In 1799, George Smith married in Newnham Murren and began working next to William King the carpenter. After George died in 1826, John Deely came from Wallingford to work in Crowmarsh Gifford next to Benjamin Dunsden the engineer. Soon after moving in the early 1850s next to Joseph Clare the wheelwright, he left, and two other shoemakers set up in Benson Lane: Thomas Gough and George Belcher. George later lived at the western end of the Bell, and after his death in 1882 there seems to have been no shoemaker until the end of the century, when Edmund Norris came to Crowmarsh Gifford. He worked at the third cottage east of the Gamecock until the Second World War. In the meantime, Albert Dawson had set up business during the First World War in Newnham, just east of what is now the post office. He traded mainly in Wallingford and used his Newnham premises for finishing. About 1927, Joseph Lay took over the business there, followed in 1962 by his former apprentice, Les Foster, with whom the tradition of local shoemaking ended.

The earliest known tailor, Thomas Smith of Newnham Murren, comes into the records for 1704. He was then unemployed with five children, and was awarded 3s a week by Quarter Sessions at Oxford. By 1841 there were three tailors, one of whom, James Debren, lived at the house that became the Gamecock. He is described as a shopkeeper in 1839, which may explain the shop-like bay window still on the house. By 1845 another tailor, Samuel Payton, had come to live next door and stayed for 15 years or more, but when James left in 1848 Charles Moss took over, having come from Mongewell where he had been a gamekeeper in the 1830s. In 1849, he too is described as a shopkeeper, but in the late 1850s he had taken his business to Benson Lane and the shop had become the Gamecock beerhouse. After Charles died, in 1883, there were no further tailors working in Crowmarsh except for a few years in the 1900s.

From about 1830, Henry Brant had a pipemaker's shop at his house in the Street next to the Gardeners Arms, followed by his son Edward in the 1860s, but the business was replaced by a carpenter's by 1877.

During the second half of the 19th century the Phillips family were limeburners as well as brick and tile makers. Their kilns were in the stone quarry adjoining Crowmarsh Hill [13]. Some time after 1853 a house and garden that had belonged to farmer John Saunders were taken over by William Phillips to set up his brick and tile merchant's business, continued as a builder's merchant by son George and grandson George Frederick, who combined it with a timber yard. Phillips sold the premises in 1947 but they remained in use as a timber yard, and since 1978 have been part of Jewsons.

A family named Smith, of Newnham Murren, were thatchers in the second half of the 19th century.

## Shopkeepers

Shops appeared in Crowmarsh in the early 19th century. By 1830 a trade directory shows that there were already four, all in Crowmarsh Street: three on the north side and one on the south.

The first to open seems to have been a bakehouse. Edward Turner was the baker, and the land tax returns show that he had been there since 1825. From a deed of 1832 [13] we can be certain that his place was at the western end of the row of houses on the north side of the Street, next to his cousin Charles Allnatt, who was living at the house known later as the Limes. By 1839, David Dearlove, a native of Hagbourne, was the baker and he was so called several times until 1851, but afterwards he became 'baker and grocer'. Presumably he had moved next door and taken on the grocer's business of the previous occupier, Adam Roberts, whose house then became divided into two, with Roberts' wife living in the eastern part in 1861. By 1863, Dearlove's shop had also become the village post office. The business stayed in the family for over a hundred years, first with David's son George, and then with George's two daughters, but they gave it up soon after the Second World War. The premises then had several uses, including a cafe, until it became a private residence in the early 1970s.

Dearlove's bakery and the Limes, early 20th century.

George Dearlove, about 1900.

Sarah, widow of Thomas Kitchen of Howbery Farm, had a general shop in 1830 at Newnham Murren, but we don't know where. It was short-lived, for nothing more is known of it. In Crowmarsh Gifford, apart from the baker, two shopkeepers are listed for 1830: William King and Richard Lewenden. Richard had come about 1827 from Newnham Murren, where he had been gamekeeper to Thomas Toovey of Newnham House. By 1839, James Copelin and James Debren were the shopkeepers. Copelin's shop was the house now known as 55 the Street. By 1852, Richard Smith, from Newnham Murren, had become the shopkeeper, but called 'grocer' by 1869, and he continued at the same place until his death in 1891. The shop passed successively to George Moss, George Honey and Isaac Wise. In 1937 it became the village post office, run by Ada Lay until 1962, but soon afterwards it changed to a private residence.

## Craftsmen and Shopkeepers

The Adam Roberts already mentioned, another native of Hagbourne, was a shopkeeper in 1841. Earlier he had been a candlemaker in Newnham (1832)[13] and then a tallowchandler in Crowmarsh Gifford (1841). He is not mentioned in an 1839 trade directory, so it seems that he opened shop about 1840. There is no further mention of him once his shop had been taken over by David Dearlove.

In the mid 1830s, David Ellen had a shop in North Stoke, but it is not known if it was the same as the grocer's opened by James Higgs at Day's Cottage in the 1840s. This shop stayed in the Higgs family until the First World War, taking on the function of a post office at the end of the 19th century. It closed in 1971.

The first known butcher was John Jacobs, who in 1841 had his shop in Newnham Murren, at the eastern end of the row of cottages (see map on page 87). There was no mention of him in 1839 so he may have opened his doors about 1840. He was soon replaced by Thomas Palmer, formerly of the Bell, but by 1851 Nathaniel Creswell had taken on the business, having been butcher in Wood Street, Wallingford. About 1870, William Dandridge, a native of Stadhampton, was the butcher, followed by his son Francis until about 1909 (see photograph on page 100), but after that it seems that Crowmarsh didn't want a butcher.

The present village shop and post office was opened in 1946 by William Goshawk, who was followed in 1955 for 22 years by Tony Lock.

For 50 years or so, from about 1875, James Guttridge had a photographer's shop in the Street, near the baker. He rode a tricycle to take his well-known pictures of the area, some of which are used in this book. He put his 'magic lantern' to good use at evening entertainments in the schoolroom.

In medieval times there used to be a market at Crowmarsh, to the detriment of Wallingford, so the burgesses claimed. When king Henry II granted a charter to Wallingford in 1155, following the war with king Stephen, he prohibited the market [14]. Perhaps such harsh treatment resulted from the part played by Crowmarsh in his humiliation at the hands of Stephen. Nevertheless, in 1214 king John had to prohibit the market again, and in 1228 the burgesses were still complaining [15]. However, a jury of 12 said on oath that since the time of Henry II the men of Crowmarsh were accustomed to sell beer and food to passers-by, as well as hay and oats. Indeed, the Earl Marshall himself, who then held the manor from the king, appeared in court and said that he did not claim a market of any sort, only the right to sell food and drink to those who lodged there. It was also recognised that the men of Crowmarsh had no oven and could not sell flesh. Morever, the burgesses said that they had the right to buy and resell in Wallingford any bread and ale sold by the men of Crowmarsh! Perhaps the hospitality to passers-by had been abused at times, to the annoyance of Wallingford. Anyway, things didn't seem to improve straightaway, for in 1234 brewing vessels were carried off to Wallingford, and in 1268 king Henry III had to prohibit the market again [16]. Nothing more is known until 1341, when it was stated that there was no market in Crowmarsh [17].

# 9. Services

People throughout the country have come to be dependent upon the service industries, and Crowmarsh is no exception.

Transport in early days was a matter of private enterprise. On the road, the local carrier or carter ran a regular service. William Watters, who lived at Crowmarsh Gifford, was a carrier for many years in the mid 19th century. Every Monday, Wednesday and Friday he followed a round trip that took him through Abingdon, Faringdon and Highworth (near Swindon). Eventually he gave up travelling, for in 1869 he is described as a grocer, and he also kept the Bell. In the early part of the 20th century the local carrier was Thomas Tucker, and he was followed by Dennis Andrews of Wallingford. Services improved with the use of motor transport. In 1928, William Wixen passed through twice a week to provide a service between Wallingford, Nettlebed, Nuffield and Stoke Row.

Few villagers travelled much before the 19th century. Not many had their own transport to get about, unless they were rich enough to have horses or a carriage; they walked. Stagecoaches, however, provided a useful means of getting about. They ran between Wallingford and London from the early 18th century, and in the 19th century passengers could travel by coach three times a week to London and daily to Reading and Oxford. When railways were introduced people became more mobile. Early in the 20th century a horse-drawn bus owned by the Lamb, Wallingford, picked up passengers for Wallingford station if ordered in advance. But road travel became much easier as regular bus services were introduced after the First World War between Oxford, Henley and Wallingford, with connections to Reading.

Until road and rail transport improved, barge traffic on the Thames was very important. Downstream of Wallingford bridge there had been a ferry in medieval times [1]; it was re-established at Chalmore Hole in 1787, when the horse towpath was laid down; it crossed here from the Oxfordshire side to Berkshire. The toll was 2d a horse [2]. The ferry boat was hailed by a bell from the Oxfordshire bank, although for a time it was worked across on a chain. It operated until 1953 although already by 1938 the Thames Conservancy were proposing to close the ferry [3].

Improved postal services followed in the wake of better transport. Wallingford operated a local penny post from 1812 onwards, well before the start of the

Village carrier in Crowmarsh Street, with Francis Dandridge outside his butcher's shop, about 1880.

national penny post in 1840. The service was good. In 1830, letters arrived at Wallingford by a foot postman from Benson every morning at half past seven and were despatched every night at nine o'clock. About 1910, a postman on his early round out from Wallingford, calling at North Stoke and Ipsden, earned 2s 6d for the five and a half hours that it took, with his exact time of arrival at each village post office entered on the appropriate GPO form. Letters from all parts of Crowmarsh went through Wallingford, though from the 1930s those from North Stoke were going through Oxford. By 1923, Crowmarsh Gifford Parish Council considered a village telephone was necessary, so an application for one was then made to the Post Office [3].

Amenities supplied by public service utilities had slight impact until the 20th century. Until then, for instance, people in Crowmarsh were heavily dependent upon tube wells for water. Some, like those at Mongewell, took their supplies from the lake. Then in 1903 Crowmarsh Gifford Parish Council agreed to let the Goring and Streatley Gas and Water Company carry their mains across Wallingford bridge and through Crowmarsh. By the 1920s the South Oxfordshire Gas and Water Company had also laid on piped water from their reservoir at Woodcote to the rest of the parish.

Crowmarsh Rural District Council had powers to see that safe water was available. In February 1916, for example, they ordered John Crook to close his bad well and connect his cottage to the mains supply. Forty years on they were still concerned with safe water, for in 1956 they were mapping all deep wells and underground workings to assess the possibility of emergency supplies in case of contamination by nuclear explosions [4].

There was a pump that stood in Crowmarsh Street outside the bakehouse until it became unfit for use at the end of the 19th century [3].

The provision of mains drainage came much later than mains water. In 1961 a scheme was proposed for

Crowmarsh but the County Council did not carry out the work until 1967, when it also enabled house-building schemes, such as the Newnham Croft estate, to go ahead [5]. Sewerage had been quite a problem at times. The boundary ditch dividing Newnham Murren from Crowmarsh Gifford in the Street took rain water from the roadway, but it was also sometimes polluted by drains from houses. In 1895, for example, there was a complaint that blood was draining into the ditch from Francis Dandridge's butcher's shop [6]. Next year the ditch was covered, at a cost of £35 10s, and the water piped through. At Mongewell, sewage from a cess-pit at the rectory was polluting the drinking water in 1908 and making the family ill [7]. At North Stoke, in 1950, bucket toilets were still being emptied once a week by a Council lorry [8]. When post-war plans were made in 1942, the estimated cost of providing sewers in Crowmarsh was £6100 [3]. Mains drainage is still proposed for North Stoke and Ipsden, but not before 1993, and at a cost of £1 million.

To begin with, gas supply was usually the responsibility of limited companies or municipal undertakings. The first company began in 1812, but small gas works could be set up without statute, and in the latter part of the 19th century both Mongewell Park and Howbery Park had private supplies. Crowmarsh Gifford and Newnham Murren had a general gas supply in 1907, when Wallingford Corporation extended their gas main across the bridge as far as the Gardeners Arms [3]. 1971 saw the conversion to North Sea gas.

Electricity was available in Crowmarsh before the Second World War, but it was some time before it was widely installed. Crowmarsh Gifford school, for example, did not have electricity until 1948 and Mongewell school even later, in 1960. Street lighting by electricity began in Crowmarsh in 1960 after a chequered history. The first lighting scheme was proposed in 1895, and in the following year Crowmarsh Street, between the bridge and Clack's Lane, was lit by paraffin oil lamps, paid for by voluntary subscription [3]. Mark Wickens, the constable, secured the job of lamplighter and lamp cleaner. In 1911, George Phillips suggested an improved street lighting scheme by gas. Major George Walsh, of Newnham House, offered to defray the cost of erecting ten gas lamps along the Street as a gesture to commemorate the coronation of king George V [3], and the work was duly carried out. In 1936, Crowmarsh Gifford Parish Council wanted to get an estimate for electric street lighting but a vote taken at a public meeting was in favour of retaining gas. At another meeting in 1945 the majority of people were still in favour of a gas scheme. At this time, North Stoke objected to paying towards any form of street lighting in other parts of the parish because they thought that lighting was not necessary in North Stoke [3]. By the late 1950s, however, the existing gas lamps had become worn out and in 1960 it was decided, at last, to convert the street lighting to electricity.

Crowmarsh Street, looking west, early 20th century.

# 10. Sick and Poor

In the 12th century a leper hospital was established in Crowmarsh, under the control of the burgesses of Wallingford [1]. It was typical of the two hundred or so medieval hospitals in England, being just outside the town boundary. The hospital's position can be deduced with some precision from two Reading Abbey charters of about 1220, both referring to lands in Newnham given to the Abbey by Richard Morin and his son William [2]. From them we can be sure that it lay in Crowmarsh Gifford parish (not in Newnham Murren as sometimes stated in later references [3]), and we can infer that it was in the part of the parish south of the Street. Presumably it was sited where the land was not liable to flooding, and must therefore have been near present-day Bridge Villa. The charters also show that it was near Tidgeon Way, which lay on or near present-day Watery Lane. The hospital was dedicated to St Mary Magdalene and it was closely associated with the hospital of St John the Baptist on the southern side of Wallingford. Its site may well explain the curious extension of the boundary of Crowmarsh Gifford ecclesiastical parish on the south side of the Street

The earliest reference to the hospital is in 1142, when Empress Matilda gave it lands in the royal manor of Benson [4]. Funds for a hospital were generally started by an endowment, usually derived from the rents of land or houses. It is possible that Matilda was the foundress; 1142 is the same year she escaped from Oxford castle to the safety of Wallingford.

Alms and grants helped to keep the hospital going. There is an early example from the reign of king Edward I (undated, but about 1280), in which John Huberd of Wallingford pledged a grant of one acre of arable land in the north field of Newnham 'to the leprous brethren and sisters of the hospital of St Mary Magdalene, of Crawmersse, in pure and perpetual arms, for his soul and for the souls of his father and mother, and of his predecessors and successors' [5]. One Alan of Banbury, by his will of 1311, gave 6d to the hospital [6]. The master, or warden, of the hospital was also the chaplain, for it was a religious foundation and it had a chapel attached to it. In 1232, an oak tree had been given for making shingles to cover the chapel of the hospital [7]. We know the names of some of the wardens. In 1317 it was Miles and it is recorded that in his capacity as warden he had received arrears of wheat due from Oving, in Buckinghamshire [4]. At times the hospital received royal attention. When Henry III visited Wallingford in December 1226 he gave the master and brethren letters of protection; and when in August 1227 he was again at Wallingford he granted full protection to the tenants and to property of every kind belonging to the hospital. He also gave directions to his subjects to receive messengers from the hospital kindly, and to 'bestow on them their substance'[8].

Lepers were probably not the only sick people to be looked after in the hospital. Leprosy was rampant in the 12th and 13th centuries, but thereafter it abated and became rare by the 15th century. So it was likely that, as happened elsewhere, the hospital was used for victims of plague and the sweating sickness, an acute, infectious fever characterised by profuse sweating, widespread in Europe during the late 15th century. By the mid 16th century the hospital function had declined and the place became known as a 'free chapel or hospital'. After Henry VIII dissolved monastic establishments, Crowmarsh hospital passed in succession to various local inhabitants: in 1557 to Edward Skinner, then of Benson; in 1577 to Walter

Hildesley of Howbery; and in 1593 to John Higgs of South Stoke [9]. The last known reference is from 1623, when it was sold to John Gregory of Wallingford along with Howbery Farm [10].

The Black Death reached England in 1348, eventually to kill about one third of the total population. Mongewell at this time had so few people left it was granted tax relief of one third [11]. Earlier in the century, in 1316, we know that some other form of pestilence had struck, killing 28 people in Wallingford gaol in little over two months, including John Gul and Peter White from Crowmarsh [12].

When plague broke out in Crowmarsh in 1671, Wallingford adopted a practical way of confining its spread. A statute of 7 December 1671 says 'wardens were set at the great bridge to keep all Crowmarsh and Newnham people out of Wallingford, which continued until the 14th day of March then next after, for there died of the plague in the two parishes sixteen persons of men, women and children, in three months, and then ceased (thanks be given to God) but many others were sick and infected there, with sores, whereof some did break and others had great swellings arising about their bodies and did sink again and not break, and yet did recover their health again. And through God's mercy our town of Wallingford was preserved' [13].

In more recent times, infectious diseases like diphtheria had to be coped with by the community. Sometimes a house was turned into a temporary isolation hospital: an example was in March 1896, when Evelyn Burden of the school house in Crowmarsh Gifford fell ill with diphtheria [14]. She died. In the same month there was a scarlet fever epidemic in Crowmarsh, and an empty cottage was fitted out as a hospital and two nurses were engaged. When there were serious outbreaks of diphtheria or measles the schools were closed. An isolation hospital was built in 1904 in St George's Road, Wallingford. A plan for it to be at Crowmarsh Hill was dropped.

'Wardens were set up at the great bridge to keep all Crowmarsh and Newnham people out of Wallingford. . .'

After an outbreak of scarlet fever at Mongewell rectory in 1908, Crowmarsh Rural District Council decided to inspect the premises. The water supply was found to be unwholesome, polluted by sewage and unfit for drinking. The house itself was in a very dirty and dilapidated condition, and had an unpleasant smell. It was in urgent need of thorough cleansing; ceilings of many rooms were almost black and paper was peeling from the walls. A w.c. on the first floor was without water and in an eminently insanitary condition [15]. Not surprisingly, the children were found to be pale and anaemic.

For a while, North Stoke folk were able to make use of a dental clinic which was set up in 1913 at the village hall by Charles Hatt, from Wallingford [16].

So the sick were looked after, to a greater or lesser extent, and so too were the poor. Parish relief, in the form of a poor rate, was implemented in the 16th century, when Overseers of the Poor were appointed to supervise endowments and charitable funds and to assess which inhabitants would have to contribute. Overseers were often churchwardens or substantial landowners, and most payers were farmers or landowners. Agricultural workers, otherwise wholly dependent on their wages, had them supplemented by grants from the poor rates.

The rates fluctuated. In 1741, for instance, as a result of a severe winter, the poor rate was raised in every parish in a sample of 25 in Oxfordshire. In the early part of the 19th century, Crowmarsh Gifford, Newnham Murren and North Stoke had higher rates levied than the average for the county. In 1803, this was 4s 8d in the pound, whereas at Crowmarsh Gifford it was 6s 2½d, at North Stoke 6s 4d, and at Newnham Murren as much as 7s 6½d [17]. Mongewell was different, as we shall see. Apart from regular payments by the Overseers, for instance to widows, money was given for burials, shoes, clothing. faggots, apprenticeships, marriage expenses, lying in, nursing, fares and so on [18].

Anyone coming to a parish and living there for at least 40 days was regarded as being settled there, and had the right to claim relief from the poor rates if need be. But if they had no prospect of work, they could be removed to their home parish by the Overseers of the Poor, acting on orders from two Justices of the Peace. The Oxford Quarter Sessions records include several such orders relating to Crowmarsh. Some removals were short-range: in 1704, for example, Thomas Smith and his five children were ordered to go from Newnham Murren to Crowmarsh Gifford [19]. He was the tailor already referred to on page 94.

In 1834, the Poor Law Amendment Act abolished parish relief for people in their own homes, but those unable to support themselves were accepted into workhouses. Parishes were encouraged to combine into Unions to provide workhouses, and the four parishes of Crowmarsh came under the Wallingford Union, along with 22 others. John Pittman King, of Rectory Farm, who lived in North Stoke until his death in 1920, was well known for his work in administering poor relief and he was chairman of the Wallingford Board of Guardians for 46 years [20].

Poor people were sometimes fortunate enough to have private help from local benfactors. Widow Anne Clack, in her will of 1594, left to every poor householder in Crowmarsh Gifford who had no corn growing of their own, one peck of wheat and one peck of malt. (A peck was equal to two gallons.) When Ralph Warcopp, of English Farm (now in Stoke Row parish), died in 1605 he left 20 nobles (one noble was 6s 8d) towards setting the poor of Newnham Murren parish at work on 'hempen wool' - hemp fibres to make a coarse yarn.

Shute Barrington, whose country home was at Mongewell Park from 1770 to 1826, was greatly concerned with the welfare of the poor. He established a village shop in which farm labourers, and all the other poor of the neighbourhood, bought whatever they wanted at a reduced price. Arthur Young, in his travels around Oxfordshire, observed: 'The wives and daughters of the cottagers receive all the flax they please, which is given them to spin into thread, and when they return such thread they are paid the full price for spinning it. The bishop has it woven into cloth, according to the fineness of the spinning, and this is sold to the cottagers' families at 2d a yard lower than the ordinary price.' Barrington made sure that cottages were built with good gardens so that his workers could grow vegetables and keep pigs. He also gave them each a stock of bees. As a result, families seldom needed relief from the parish [17]. In 1803, when, as we have seen, Crowmarsh Gifford, Newnham Murren and North Stoke all levied high poor rates, Mongewell's rate was below the county average, at only 4s 3d. Barrington himself even continued paying poor rates on his beechwoods, although they were in fact exempted, because he disapproved of such exemption![17]

Shute Barrington, who looked after his parishioners so well, was only one of many to establish charities to ensure the continuing welfare of the poor. In 1809, he set up funds for the maintenance and support of a free school at Mongewell, to place poor children in apprenticeships, and to support the village shop; and if there was any money left over it was to go to benefit poor cottagers [21]. The shop has long since gone and the school is now part of a house, but the Barrington Charity still exists, though in altered form to meet changing needs. Of recent years the money has been administered under the name of Mongewell Charity for the Poor, and has been used for practical help in the form of goods such as coal and grocery vouchers. Funds from the Charity also entitled the sick of Mongewell to a free bed in Wallingford Cottage Hospital.

Providing bread was a favoured form of charity. In Crowmarsh Gifford, in the middle of the 18th century, there was a fund known as Mary Bigg's gift, which provided £1 1s yearly to the churchwardens for distribution of bread to the poor on Christmas Eve [22]. This charity was apparently the same as that known as Elizabeth Cottingham's Charity. (Elizabeth Cottingham before marriage was Elizabeth Bigg, daughter of Mary Bigg.) Unfortunately it lapsed about 1850 when the land involved, which gave rent to the fund, was sold and mention of the gift was omitted from the deeds of conveyance [23]. When Robert Dorrell of North Stoke died in 1753 he left 5s a year to be given to the poor in bread or cakes [24]. This was paid out for about 40 years, but the poor were not then left to go without, for Thomas Dodd in 1803 left provision in his will for a charity to give £5 for bread, to be distributed every Christmas Day to the poor of North Stoke by the minister and churchwardens. This charity benefitted many: in 1935 it was recorded that 118 recipients had extra loaves because bread had been cheaper in the past few years and there was an accumulation in the annual balance [25].

Others gave charity in the form of cash. At the end of the 17th century, Bartholomew Smith left rent, amounting to £14 from two estates and two cottages, to poor labourers of Newnham Murren to be paid out, appropriately, on St Bartholomew's Day [26]. The aged poor and needy of Crowmarsh Gifford parish were left money by Mary and Sarah Owen in 1892, to be given out to those whom the rector considered to be the most deserving. This money is still available.

Perhaps the most well-known charity in Crowmarsh is that of William Emery. It was established in his will dated 4 April 1690. He left a cottage next to the Bell, subsequently known as Poors Cottage, and five parcels of land. After various exchanges and sales the land was consolidated into one plot, now used as allotments, to the south of the Street between Bridge Villa camp-site and Thames Mead [27]. The following is an extract from the will, with modern punctuation but original spelling.

'. . . Item, I doe likewise give, devise, limit, bequeath and appoint (unto the like charitable and pious uses herein after mentioned): all that cottage or tenement with the appurtenances in Cromarsh Gifford aforesaid (heretofore in the possession of Margaret Hall), the garden and appurtenances to the same belonging; and all those five acres and an halfe of arrable land (by estimation bee the same more or less) lying and being in the common arrable ffeilds of Crowmarsh Gifford aforesaid (hereinafter more particularly butted, bounded and expressed), that is to say, one halfe acre thereof in the Hitching ffeild in Crowmarsh Gifford aforesaid (and abutting south upon the said last mentioned cottage or tenement), two acres more thereof lyeing in Stockbridge in Cromarsh Gifford aforesaid (shooting on Stockbridge Close aforesaid, church land there south, and land of Mr Blackall north), three halfe acres more thereeof in the Hitching in Cromarsh Gifford (shooting north on Steers Lane stile, land of John Higgs west, and land of Mr Smith east), one halfe acre residue thereof lyeing under Steers Lane hedge (land heretofore of Mr

Vrlin [sic] south, and Steers Lane north). And my will and meaning is that, for ever yearely and every yeare after my decease, the rents, issues and profits of the said last mentioned cottage or tenement, and the said five acres and an halfe last mentioned, shall bee (for ever after my decease yearely and every yeare) had, received and taken, on the ffeast day of the Annunciation of Our Blessed Lady St Mary the Virgin next after my decease, by the minister, churchwardens and overseers of the poore of the parish of Nuneham Murry [sic] aforesaid for the time being (or the major parts of them) and by them (or the major parts of them), yearely and every year after my decease, given and disposed of unto and amongst the most indigent and poorest people of the said parish of Nuneham Murry aforesaid, on the ffeast day of Pentecost (commonly called Whitsunday). Item . . .'

Nowadays the money is used for a range of benefits to any people with particular needs. The main income is from the fees for the allotments.

An interesting sideline about this charity is a tradition that Emery had found a buried hoard on a plot where he farmed below Berin's Hill, in Ipsden [28]; at his death he was indeed a rich man.

When Emery made his will his wife had already died, and having no children of his own he made legacies to his maid servant, Mary Alden, and to various kinfolk, including the three daughters of his half-sister's son, William Marks of Ipsden. The residue was to be equally divided among his four executors. He gave his will to Mary Alden, charging her to keep it and to give it personally to his attorney, Richard Blackall of Wallingford. In his last sickness, Emery wanted to change his will, so he called for Blackall. But he too was ill, and when at last he could come Emery was so weak he was afraid to make alterations lest he would not have the strength to hear the new will read. Emery wept at the thought of possible trouble between the legatees and his four executors, who included Marks and a youth, Anthony,

# Sick and Poor

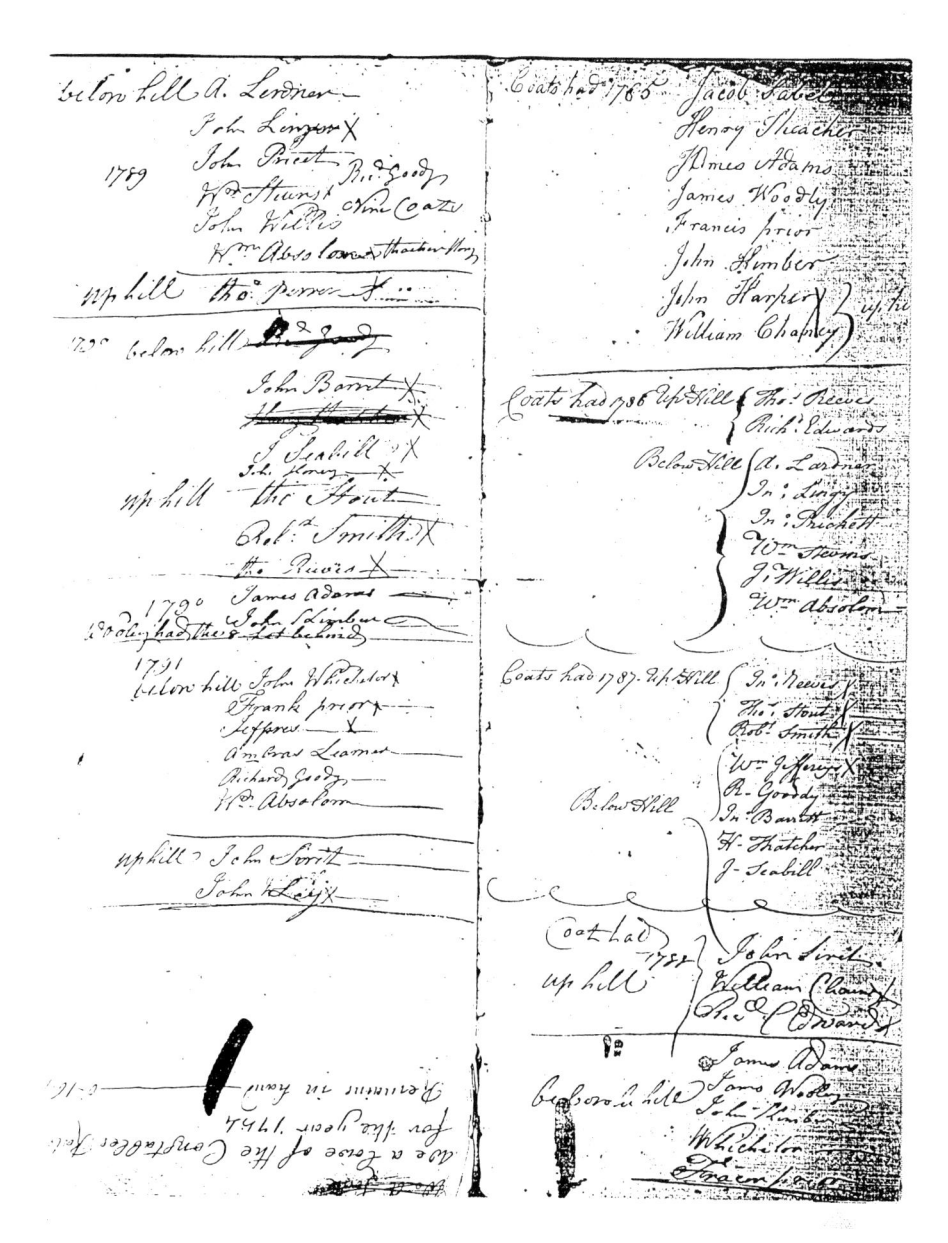

Extract from Newnham Murren churchwardens' account book showing the names of some poor parishioners who received great coats, 1785-1791, from William Emery's will. (Courtesy of Crowmarsh Gifford PCC.)

son of Anthony Day of Newnham Farm. His apprehension was justified by subsequent events.

After the executors had seen Emery buried at Hampsted Norreys on 13 June 1691 and paid the funeral expenses, they had an inventory of his goods drawn up two days later. It amounted to some £2,500, almost all of which was in bonds and mortgages owed by about 80 people. The papers were put in a locked trunk in a locked room in Emery's house. Marks had the trunk key, and young Day the room key, and the four executors agreed not to meddle without the consent of all of them. But whilst three were in London on 1 July proving the will, Day (who was too young to assist in the proving) stole the trunk (with the assent of the other two executors, it was later claimed by Marks) and took it to Newnham Farm, where it was broken open. He justified this move by claimimg (contrary to the will) that Emery had told his relations and neighbours that a quarter of his estate would be settled on Day, not a quarter of the residue after settling of debts and legacies; and that this had been put in writing and entered into Emery's long book, although on inspection this was found to be so defaced as to be unreadable. Moreover, the other two executors claimed that Marks had planned to get the whole estate.

The counter accusations about the division of Emery's estate led to several suits in Chancery from 1691 to 1694, and it is from the court records that we get the details of the squabbling [29], which included threats of prolonged and expensive litigation which might be avoided if the other two executors would sell their shares for £250 apiece! On 19 January 1693, the court ordered that all the parties should account for the monies that they had received, and the whole estate should be brought 'into hotchpot', i.e. into court where it could be divided equally between the executors after the legacies had been paid. This was done, but suits continued and the final outcome is unknown.

## Sick and Poor 115

Small charities exist for the upkeep of church buildings at Crowmarsh Gifford and Newnham Murren [30], and Crowmarsh has also benefitted from the Wallingford Bridge Estate Charity. In 1981, for instance, £200 each was donated for Crowmarsh Gifford church organ and for Crowmarsh village hall [31].

Income from Crowmarsh parish has in turn been used to help the needy elsewhere. Stephen Field, in his will of 1727, left seven acres in Crowmarsh Gifford, the rent from which was to be distributed among the poor of Iffley and Littlemore. William Emery similarly bequeathed some rents to go to the poor of Hampsted Norreys.

Not a charitable trust, but one raising large sums of money for charity in recent years, is the Crowmarsh-based Giffords Concert Party. Among those who have benefitted from their enthusiasm and hard work have been local scouts and brownies, the football and cricket clubs, as well as hospitals. Charity in Crowmarsh is indeed alive and well.

Crowmarsh Street, early 20th century.

# 11. Recreation

What did people in Crowmarsh do for recreation? To start with, the annual fair must have been a great event to look forward to. For centuries a great fair was kept in Crowmarsh Gifford. Medieval fairs were important occasions, vital for supplying largely self-supporting communities with such things as salt, clay pots, millstones and iron for implements, and for selling animals and the hiring of labour; new laws were proclaimed there too. In the Middle Ages the fair at Crowmarsh Gifford was said to have been the most considerable in the county. It took place on the feast day of St Mary Magdalene, changing from 22 July to 2 August in 1753, after the Gregorian calendar was introduced. One of the stall holders in 1690 was William Emery, founder of the Emery charity.

The king could grant the right of tolls of fairs, and each fair was regularised by a charter, although the one for Crowmarsh seems not to have survived. At one time Crowmarsh fair belonged to the son of Edward III, the Black Prince [1]. The lord of the manor had the right to the tolls, which changed hands as manors were sold and bought [2]. Fairs weren't always a pleasure for some, however. In 1340, during the reign of Edward III, there was an enquiry into an affray at Crowmarsh fair in which armed men assaulted the merchants, plundering their goods, and killing a man named Robert Cailly [1]. These men had apparently travelled around from fair to fair in the county with evil intent.

Affray at Crowmarsh Fair in 1340, when Robert Cailly was murdered.

During the 19th century, as shops became more common, the fair lost much of its commercial function; it declined and became used only for the sale of livestock and for pleasure. By the 1860s it had become just a horse fair, with dealing taking place in the orchard of the Bell, but with some stalls still lining the Street [3].

From time to time there were local festivities which broke the monotony of daily work. In the last hundred years in particular, we have a written record of many of the events that took place.

Jubilees and coronations and royal weddings were celebrated enthusiastically. Mongewell school generously gave its pupils a whole week's holiday to mark Queen Victoria's golden jubilee in 1887, and a few more days holiday when it came to her diamond jubilee [4]. In Crowmarsh Gifford and Newnham Murren, tea and amusements were provided to mark the diamond jubilee. The 1902 and 1911 coronations were typically celebrated with tea and distribution of meat and mugs [5]. For the coronation of George V in 1911 the folk of Mongewell got together with those of North Stoke, thanks to the generosity of Alexander Fraser of Mongewell Park, who paid for the parishioners' day out. Dinner and tea were provided in John Wormald's barn near the mill, and there was an afternoon of sports. It was noted at the time that 'perhaps the most exciting item was the ladies' hobble skirt race' [6]! Queen Elizabeth's silver jubilee in 1977 was celebrated in the traditional way, with mugs for all the children and games and tea.

Peace celebrations also brought everyone together. On hearing the news of the fall of Pretoria in June 1900, towards the close of the Boer War, the children of Crowmarsh Gifford and Newnham Murren improvised a day of singing and races, and collected money for a special tea. In 1919, after the end of the First World War, Mongewell folk again went to North Stoke to celebrate. They joined in a day of sports, feasting and dancing. Dinner was served in the village hall, and to mark the occasion Clara Butt sang grace and 'Rule Britannia' [7].

The grounds of Howbery Park were for many years opened in the summer for people to come and enjoy themselves. Early in the 20th century the Park was used for agricultural shows. It was a popular place for school outings, too. One day in August 1869, 340 children had a Sunday school treat there [8]. The grounds of Newnham House were likewise used for festive occasions. Flower shows were held there for many years at the turn of the century. Sometimes the children went there for their school treats, and in July 1901 Alexander Fraser paid for the Mongewell children to attend the temperance fete held there [4]. At the 1899 temperance fete some four thousand people came to Newnham House and enjoyed, among other things, a trapeze artist (Professor Fleet!) and a hot air balloon and parachute descent. The parachutist apparently landed in Alfred de Mornay's standing wheat off Benson Lane [9].

Crowmarsh continued to have a fete from time to time, then after a lapse it was revived in 1967, taking place in the Benson Lane village hall and grounds [10]. In 1971 and 1972 the venue was the Cox's Lane football field. During the last ten years Crowmarsh Gifford school has drawn the crowds to its own summer fete.

Various sporting activities have been available. A flourishing football club has been running since 1963. There were village teams in existence at the beginning of the century, too. In 1982 Crowmarsh cricket club reformed after being defunct for almost 30 years. Again, there had been village elevens early in the century. And North Stoke started a tennis club in 1928. Swimming, boating and fishing in the Thames were close at hand. Pony races were held on Great Meadow in the mid 19th century. More recently, horse riding has been available at Blenheim Riding Centre. In the 1970s, horses were also ridden out from the field next to Wallingford camp-site, though there were complaints about the very bad state of Watery Lane bridleway because it was so churned up by heavy use.

Start of an outing to celebrate VE Day.

Rifle shooting was popular in Edwardian times. In 1903, rifle practice took place at Crowmarsh Gifford rectory. Then in 1906 a rifle club was started in the disused chalk pit at the side of Crowmarsh Hill, and competitions were held with other villages. On winter evenings, practice was in the infants' school!

In 1908, a 9-hole golf course was laid out on the meadows at Newnham Murren, and was used into the 1920s. Play was subject to interruption by flooding, however, like in December 1910 when the links were under three to four feet of water.

Many other clubs have been organised, for adults and children alike. Some are now defunct but others have flourished and catered for all sorts of interests in the community. In 1965 the Crowmarsh Area Social Benevolent Society was formed, with the purpose of fund-raising for donations to organisations, and sometimes individuals. Regular bingo sessions, competitions and so on were held. It closed in 1979 after financial difficulties, but one of its activities continued - the 'Friendly Neighbours' club for elderly people.

Women's Institutes have played an important part in village life. The North Stoke WI was established in 1917 to help the war effort, and had Clara Butt for its first president [11]. Crowmarsh WI came later, in 1941; it too was founded to help with the war effort and to give women a place to relax and discuss their problems. Miss Morrell of Newnham Croft was its first president and, to start with, meetings were held in Miss Florence Brown's garden room at the Giffords. During the war years, garden fetes to raise funds were held at Newnham Croft [12].

Finding a suitable place for activities wasn't always easy. Sir John Wormald of the Springs built North Stoke village hall in 1911 as a memorial to king Edward VII. The site was the orchard attached to Kimberley Cottage. It cost £1000. Before that time, the Parish Room, formerly the school, was used for meetings, but it was rather small. By the 1950s, however, the hall was little used and it was largely neglected until 1967, when it was extended and improved and formally reopened [13]. Crowmarsh Gifford and Newnham Murren did not get a hall until later, when after many years of fund-raising a hall comprising three ex-army huts was put up by voluntary labour in the early 1950s. It was opened for use in 1954 and gave good service until replaced in 1976 [14].

The quest for a suitable recreation ground in Crowmarsh has kept parish councillors busy for nigh on a hundred years. In 1896, Crowmarsh Gifford Parish Council had discussed the provision of a public recreation ground, but nothing was resolved. By the 1930s a serious search began, and local landowners were approached. Many sites were proposed but all were rejected. The main difficulty encountered was the unwillingness of landowners to sell land, compounded by the uncertainty of the route of the proposed Crowmarsh by-pass. A site was very nearly available in 1938, when the sale of five acres of the field to the rear of the District Council offices was negotiated. The National Playing Fields Association offered a grant of £300. Unfortunately, in 1940 the offer of the grant was withdrawn owing to the national emergency and the whole scheme was shelved. By 1982, Crowmarsh Parish Council still considered the provision of a playing field an absolute priority. A suitable piece of land immediately south of the school was sought, but unsuccessfully. Neither was there any success for another bid in 1987 for the site mooted in 1938.

A small children's play area was meanwhile created out of the church allotments, between Thames Mead and the Bridge Villa camp-site, with the Parochial Church Council leasing the land to the Parish Council. The area is known as 'Billy's Field', named after a pony that had been kept there.

The Crowmarsh Boys' Football Club was able to use the small playing field owned by the developers,

Messrs Pye, in Cox's Lane, but in 1976 it began using the North Stoke recreation ground, where there was a better pitch and a new pavilion. The North Stoke ground had been given to the village by Sir Alexander Condie Stephen in 1896 in exchange for a strip of land adjoining the mill stream. The land exchange deed stated that this area of land would be a greater benefit to the inhabitants in that it was 'far better adapted for use as a recreation ground being much larger, high, dry, more compact in shape and not liable to floods as the land to be given up by the Parish' [15].

Inns and beerhouses have long been meeting places. Crowmarsh folk had a choice.

The Bell has been an inn since at least 1742, although there was no alehouse in Crowmarsh Gifford in 1687 [16]. In the 17th century, the house, even if not then an inn, may well have been among the Crowmarsh properties of Walter Bigg that passed to his son David and so to his grandson Richard, for Richard's property in Crowmarsh Gifford, sold by the executors of his daughter Elizabeth Cottingham to William Blackstone in 1763, included the Bell [17]. Walter's wealth may have come at least in part from brewing, for he had two brewhouses at his death in 1659. In 1845, Sir William Blacksone's grandson sold his Crowmarsh property to his cousin the Revd Harry Lee, who is named as owner of the Bell in the tithe award schedule of that year, but he mortgaged it in 1852 to James Morrison of Basildon House. Because the mortgage was apparently in default, the inn stayed with the Morrison family until its sale to Morlands in 1910 [18].

The house seems to have been sublet, for in the 1786 land tax returns the 'owner' is named as Mrs Holmes, presumably the widow of Thomas Holmes. A Sarah Holmes, presumably their daughter, married Charles Palmer in 1783, and they took over the house as 'owner' from 1788, and also as 'occupier' from 1801. Their son Thomas was there until the early

1840s - a family tenancy of over 50 years. There was another long tenancy in the second half of the 19th century, when the innkeeper was William Watters and then his widow Elizabeth, both of whom also had a grocer's business - perhaps innkeeping wasn't too profitable.

The Queens Head is an early 14th century house. Its east end shows it is an 'aisled hall' - having a frame broad enough for the roof to need support from two lines of posts as well as from the walls. In 1697, when it was sold by John Blackall of Crowmarsh Gifford to Thomas Sarney, blacksmith of Newnham Murren, it was known as the Three Cocks. It passed to Thomas's daughter, Ann Hurst, who sold it to Richard Spyer of Berrick Salome in 1767, when it had come to be known by its present name. After a further sale in 1789 to Edward Wells, brewer of Wallingford, it passed to the Wallingford Brewery Company, and then in 1963 to Ushers [19].

Early 20th century. Poors Cottage is behind the inn sign.

At the corner of Benson Lane and the Street is a house with a Morland's Brewery sign. It was built as a beerhouse about 1830 for Daniel Grant, who had been coachman to Shute Barrington of Mongewell Park. In 1826, bishop Barrington had left £100 in his will to Grant, who in that year bought the corner site, but sold it with the house in 1833 [20]. By then the beerhouse keeper was John Brant, who stayed until his death in 1847. Next year, his widow, Ann, had the house, and it is then that we hear that it was known as the Coach and Horses, presumably because of Grant's occupation. At the 1851 census the house was occupied by farmer George Absolon. Around the corner, next to Howbery Farm, lived Thomas Nailer, a gardener from Bucklebury, Berkshire, and by the next year he had become the beerseller. He stayed there until about 1877. By 1881, Thomas Lovegrove had the house, staying there until at least 1911, by which time the name Gardeners Arms had come into use. These two tenancies were long, but they were outrun by the last, that of Robert Merrison, and later his widow Ethel, who between them had the house until it closed for the sale of beer in 1967 [21].

The bay-windowed Gamecock Cottage was a beerhouse for a hundred years. First mention of a beerseller was in the census of 1861. After finally passing to the Wallingford and Henley Brewery, the Gamecock closed about 1959.

The White House has been a public house or inn for North Stoke since it was built about 1845.

Parish magazines of one sort or another have kept folk in touch with local news for most of the last hundred years. In 1908, the vicar of North Stoke, Herbert Coombes, began a magazine for North Stoke, Ipsden and Mongewell which continued until 1937. It initially cost one penny. Some years earlier, in 1898, the rector of Crowmarsh Gifford, Albert Dams, had begun one, written by himself and continued until 1909, when he moved to Goring. He was a very conscientious and hard working man with a strong literary turn of mind. John Dale subsequently kept various notes and a 'parish paper' going in Crowmarsh Gifford and Newnham Murren between 1925 and 1949.

The Crowmarsh Chronicle was begun in 1966 as an enterprise by the Crowmarsh Area Social Benevolent Society, with an initial circulation of nearly 250 copies, price 6d. It was followed in 1978 by the Crowmarsh News, partly financed from the parish rate and distributed free to all parishioners.

Early 14th century timber frame of the Queen's Head.

# 12. Law and Order

Not all Crowmarsh folk have been law-abiding. In 1323, the abbot of Rewley, Oxford, complained that men from Crowmarsh - Thomas Aleyn, Nicholas the cooper, Roger Acverd, Thomas Jonesson the reeve, John Randolf and John at Forty, along with Roger at Rush of Newnham and Walter Loveday of Mongewell, among others - broke and burnt his houses at Nettlebed and Benson, felled his trees and carried away his trees and other goods [1]. (Forty is the name of the meadow just south of Wallingford bridge and west of Watery Lane.) Their punishment is unknown but one early sentence we do know about was at the end of the 13th century, when criminal charges were brought against Hugh the miller of Mongewell by an informer named Henry of Bakewell. The miller was brought to the gaol at Wallingford castle and afterwards hanged [2]. Much later, a Crowmarsh woman named Sarah Exlade was more fortunate: at the Oxford assizes in February 1772 she was charged with the murder of her bastard daughter but she was acquitted [3].

In medieval times, someone accused of a serious crime could seek sanctuary in the church, to avoid unlawful retribution and to await a proper trial. For example, the eyre rolls (of justices in circuit) of 1241 record that Henry, son of Geoffrey of Crowmarsh, fled after knifing Ralph le Poer in the belly so that he died; and Henry's sister Alice took sanctuary in Crowmarsh church, admitting she was a party to the death.

# Law and Order

All manner of crimes perpetrated in Crowmarsh, such as murder, riot, assault and theft, were heard in the courts at Oxford as the Quarter Sessions records show. For many criminals the punishment was very severe, as John Harrison found to his cost in 1789. He was convicted of stealing silver and other valuables from William Goodall and Ann Newman of Newnham Murren, and sentenced to seven years transportation [4]. In 1773, William Fry had received double this, after first being sentenced to death for stealing a mare belonging to John Allnatt [5].

Transportation was also the sentence for Thomas and William Wadley of Crowmarsh Gifford in 1831. They were charged and found guilty, with six others, of destroying a threshing machine belonging to Thomas Newton of Crowmarsh Battle farm. Their action was part of a series of widespread riots by agricultural workers in south-eastern England protesting against low wages and the threat of unemployment. The men who led groups of rioters often made proclamations and signed threatening letters under the pseudonym of 'Captain Swing'. For their part in the Swing riots the Wadley brothers were sent to Tasmania for seven years (although they subsequently stayed on), and another Crowmarsh Gifford man was imprisoned for twelve months [6].

In 1776, when John Wicks was found guilty of stealing goods from Susan Hicks and wheat from John Allnatt's barn at Crowmarsh Farm, he was sentenced to be burnt in the hand and to suffer imprisonment for twelve months [7].

For those who had committed lesser offences there were fines or the degradation of time to be spent in the stocks. The constable of Crowmarsh Gifford reported to the Oxford Quarter Sessions in April 1700 that the stocks and whipping post were in good repair [8] - obviously ready to receive the law-breakers! We do not know what eventually became of these particular items of punishment.

Some crimes remained a mystery. How did a valuable bible belonging to North Stoke church come to be found in the rubbish pit at White Hill in February 1926? Probably it was illegally removed when the church was being restored earlier this century. Then, who burgled the church safe at North Stoke in the spring of 1936? Previously, in 1882, the parish clerk had been dismissed for stealing the offertory money! [9]

More recently, in July 1985, two criminals were brought to justice for robbing Crowmarsh post office of £1,700. The men both came from London: one was jailed for seven years and the other sentenced to five years youth custody.

One way in which peremptory justice was meted out was in the form of 'rough music'. Such an event occurred at the very end of the 19th century when a local shepherd abandoned his wife and children and went to live with an unmarried girl. The neighbours decided it was an appropriate case for rough music. This is what happened. Each evening for about a week the younger men gathered near the offending girl's home, armed with tin cans and other noisy objects, and marched past in front of the house beating the cans and making the loudest din possible. They continued to and fro for about an hour, and each time the house was passed the noise of the cans ceased just long enough for the marchers to shout 'Ba! Ba!'. The village policeman, on hearing the turmoil, took his stand in front of the house. The demonstrators, though, knew their rights and as long as they kept on the move and made no attack on the house, the arm of the law would not interfere. After the period of rough music was over, the couple decided to quit and the shepherd moved to a farm many miles away.

A violent quarrel at North Stoke in 1525 was not settled without recourse to the Court of Star Chamber, the records of which give a graphic account of the day's events [10]. On Tuesday 7 March in the 16th year of the reign of Henry VIII (i.e. 1525), Thomas

Bradshaw, vicar of North Stoke, was hedging at his parsonage when he was attacked by Roger Hatchman and others. Hatchman was wielding a long forest hook which he thrust into Bradshaw's body close to his heart so that he feared for his life. One of Hatchman's followers then got behind Bradshaw and knocked from his hand a hedging hook, the only defence he had. On seeing this, Hatchman thrust a dagger a great way under Bradshaw's armpit so that he was forced to flee. But William Bolter, who had been threshing in the barn, brought Bradshaw his bow, and two arrows were shot beside his pursuers to warn them off. Then Hatchman's wife, armed with a dagger, tried to kill Bradshaw.

All this was Bradshaw's account; Hatchman's was different, not unexpectedly. He claimed that the attack was the other way: Bradshaw and others had set upon him. He also claimed that several times his servants had been chased and attacked, including an occasion on 12 March when Bradshaw had encouraged some Oxford students to chase them in Wallingford town.

This violence, and more, had come about because of a dispute over who had the right to occupy the parsonage. In 1511, John Bolter (father of William) leased the parsonage from Bromhall Priory (for a yearly payment of 20 quarters of corn and 50 of malt [11]), but when he died the lease was forfeited because of certain commitments that had not been met. This meant that John's widow, Katherine, did not get the lease. Instead, it went to his brother, Thomas, being renewed when the parsonage passed to St John's College, Cambridge, at the dissolution of the Priory. Yet in her will of 1513, Katherine claimed to pass the lease to her brother, who in turn claimed to pass it to Hatchman. But Thomas Bolter made over his rights to Thomas Bradshaw on 5 February 1525. This clearly infuriated Hatchman, who already had several times taken away Bolter's tithe corn, valued at 150s yearly [12], and had even broken into and temporarily occupied the house whilst he was ploughing, forcing his wife and children out. Bradshaw could not have been too badly wounded for he continued as vicar of North Stoke until 1554.

As nowadays, the law stepped in when someone was found dead. On 12 January 1771, for example, John Barrett hanged himself whilst staying at a public house, and the jury at the coroner's inquest at Crowmarsh returned a verdict of lunacy. He had lived in Newnham Murren, having married there only seven years before. Jackson's Oxford Journal reported the occurrence at some length. 'He was formerly a very considerable farmer, but had failed, yet was in no wise distressed having ever since been handsomely supported by wealthy relations. On the morning of his death it appears that after leaving his bed he had dressed himself from head to foot and then tied a small string to a staple in the wall by which he was hanged. But he was found in a sloping posture, with his feet firm on the ground and his hands rested on the window frame as if he had been looking out [13].'

Keeping law and order in the parish was largely the responsibility of the local constable. He would formerly have been appointed by the manorial courts, then for a long period by the Justices of the Peace. In the mid 19th century the county police force was formed and the village policeman came into being. Crowmarsh Gifford had its own policeman for a while, but he was withdrawn about 1890 and a replacement was not made until the Parish Council petitioned the Chief Constable in 1895 [14]. Several reasons were given. To start with, Wallingford policemen did not patrol the Street. Secondly, all manner of travelling fairs, theatres, etc. located themselves on Crowmarsh meadows. Also, tramps from Wallingford Workhouse and elsewhere who passed through the village were often a nuisance to shopkeepers and residents. Moreover, with four licensed houses in the Street there were disturbances at closing time, and gambling games were openly played in the Street, by-lanes and footpaths on Sundays! A few months later Mark Wickens took up his duties. He carried a 'ground-ash' stick with which he issued summary punishment, such as when boys were caught in the act of robbing Dearlove's orchard or men were found fighting together. About 1870, another enterprising village policeman, this time at North Stoke, doubled up as the master at Sunday School [15].

The Crowmarsh Gifford village constable during the 1920s was P.C. Croughton, one of the old-fashioned type. Once on a Sunday morning he noticed a number of cars parked outside the foundry while the owners were in church; amongst them was Walter Wilder's. P.C. Croughton decided something should be done about it - but what about Mr Wilder's car? Resourcefully, he opened the gates of the foundry, pushed the car inside, closed the gates and summoned the others for obstruction!

# 13. War and Misfortune

Crowmarsh has been involved in civil conflict, though little except documentary evidence remains to show that soldiers fought in two civil wars here.

In 1066 William the Conqueror passed peacefully through Crowmarsh on his roundabout way from Hastings to Berkhamsted and thence to London, having crossed the Thames at Wallingford [1]. Less than a century later Crowmarsh was in turmoil, with king Stephen constructing a series of wooden forts opposite Wallingford Castle, in his war against the army of his cousin the Empress Matilda, who contended the throne. Chroniclers of the time have left records of the progress of this war [2].

Stephen built his first two forts in 1139. They were designed to check the marauding activities of the Wallingford garrison as a siege had proved too difficult. Whether there was a fort at Crowmarsh is unclear until 1152. In that year, Stephen attacked Wallingford for a third time, blocking access to the bridge by building a fort at the Crowmarsh end. At this time, duke Henry (Matilda's son, and later Henry II) was in Normandy raising an army, but he returned to England and reached Wallingford by the middle of 1153, when he blockaded Stephen's forts and dug trenches to prevent troops getting out. The king then brought up a large army. He was anxious for battle but the leading men in both armies shrank from further conflict and a truce was made, leading to the Treaty

# War and Misfortune

Crowmarsh siege fort was last used in 1153.

of Westminster in which Henry was named Stephen's successor. One of the terms was the destruction of the fortifications at Crowmarsh.

The details of the location of Stephen's forts are confusing and there are now no visible remnants, but they almost certainly stood in or near the field, between the church and river, that later came to be known as Barbican Close. It has been alleged that Crowmarsh Gifford church was used as a fortified post during the conflict, and desecrated [3].

Certainly the churches were not spared in the Civil War between king Charles I and Parliament, a time of much disruption and hardship in this area. The security of Oxford, held by the Royalists, depended upon maintaining an outer ring of garrisons and strongpoints. One of these was Wallingford and it was given a garrison of over 1,000 men.

Extracts from journals kept by Sir Samuel Luke, a commander under Cromwell who had a network of spies, show the difficulties of people living in constant fear of skirmishes, requisitions and plunder. For example, Sunday 28 May 1643. 'Edward Sherwyn went and returned this day from Wallingford and saith that the forces continue there still as they were yesterday and that the soldiers are in greate feare of the Lord generalls approaching thither, and that the skouts keepe watch continually in the feild neere Cromarsh, and that the country thereabouts are forced to bringe in provision or money dayly for horse, as he was certified by a tithingman whoe carried in his money thither the last night'[4].

The situation was no better nine months later. Saturday 17 February 1644. 'That the Governor of Wallingford hath comand to furnish the castle with beefe and biskitt whoe thereupon went into the castle to view the old store and it was all spoild, insoemuch that they threw away 40 hogsheads of beefe that stunke and not fitt to bee eaten, and now they search the contry for bacon and take it away and carry it into the castle. That the soldiers have noe pay, but are permitted to fetch cattle out of the contry instead of their pay'[5].

In 1643 the defences of Wallingford castle were strengthened, and the bridge was cut in four places for wooden drawbridges to be inserted. (These gaps were not restored with masonry until 1751.) A scout reported in May 1644, 'At Crowmarsh they have laid carts across the streets and cut down trees and have laid them in the way that horse cannot pass'[6].

Soon after Oxford surrendered in 1646, a parliamentary force under Captain Gibbons was sent from Henley to block up Wallingford on the Crowmarsh side. At the bridge they found and attacked a small detachment from the castle garrison stationed to secure the free passage of the bridge. Many of these soldiers were taken prisoner and the remainder were compelled to repass the bridge into the town[7].

Inside Newnham Murren church an Elizabethan brass tablet, to the memory of Lettice Barnard who died in 1593, has a bullet mark on it, said to have been made by a musket fired by one of the soldiers besieging Wallingford. Wallingford castle was subsequently surrounded and its garrison surrendered on 27 July 1646. Later, in 1649, the tenant of Rectory Farm at North Stoke at least gained some compensation: relief of rent (to £175 a year) was granted to William Dormer 'because of taxes and some damage he had received by the garrison at Oxford'[8].

The lych gate at Crowmarsh Gifford church and the sundial in North Stoke churchyard bear testimony to the men of Crowmarsh who served in the world wars of the present century. Parish magazines covering the war years help to remind us of those times. For instance, in its November 1914 issue, the North Stoke and Ipsden Parish Magazine stated that soldiers from the Honourable Artillery Company were billeted in North Stoke. They stayed for a month before leaving for the Front, and various entertainments were held for them in the village hall. The Rural District Council reported that the troops had left the footpaths in a bad condition! The same magazine gave items of news of men at the Front right through its First World War issues, as well as news of the war effort at home - the Red Cross working party busy at sewing and making crutches, the band of women formed for farm work.

Among the many brave men who sacrificed their lives was Charles Anderson. A citation recorded in a North Stoke Vestry minute book (1848-1958) reads: 'Awarded the Albert Medal, 1st class, in recognition of the gallantry of Lance-Corporal Charles Henry Anderson, late of the 1/14th Battalion of the London Regiment, who lost his life in France in saving the lives of others. On 28th of November 1916, Lance Corporal Anderson was in a hut with eleven other men, when, accidentally, the safety pin was withdrawn from a bomb. In the semi-darkness he shouted a warning to the men, rushed to the door, and endeavoured to open it so as to throw the bomb into a field. Failing to do this, when he judged that the five seconds during which the fuse was timed to burn had elapsed, he held the bomb as close to his body as possible with both hands in order to screen the other men in the hut. Anderson himself and one other man were mortally wounded by the explosion, and five men were injured. The remaining five escaped unhurt. Anderson sacrificed his life to save his comrades.'

The Berks & Oxon Advertiser for 11 February 1916 reported that a Zeppelin airship had passed over Crowmarsh and Wallingford, a close reminder of the world at war. By 1917 food shortages on the Home Front were worsening. Crowmarsh Gifford Parish Council, in common with others, was obliged to set up a committee on food economy. The council wrote to John W Edwards of Crowmarsh Farm and the other local landowners to see if any spare suitable land was available for growing food. Some extra land was offered but the shortage of farm labourers made extra allotments impracticable. Howbery meadows, however, were ploughed up in the last year of the war.

The Second World War brought many different people and changes to Crowmarsh. School children were soon affected. Crowmarsh Gifford School was host to evacuated children from St Andrew's and St Philip's LCC school at Kensington [9]. At first the school worked a double shift system with the local children and the London children each having four hours a day; but by January 1940 the two schools amalgamated for normal work, with Betty Hasthorpe in charge at the main building and Miss Plested, the LCC teacher, taking her class in the Parish Room.

In September 1939, children from Northfields School, Ealing, were billeted at Mongewell and North Stoke and nineteen of them were admitted to Mongewell School, together with another seven from other parts of London and Essex [10]. The school coped with varying numbers of evacuees until the spring of 1945. The school log book records the preparations in event of enemy attack - time off for children to be fitted with their gas masks, buying blackout material and wire meshing to cover windows. It records, too, the date when school dinners were first introduced - 29 September 1942 - and the efforts of the children to 'do their bit', such as the time in January 1943 when some of them had collected £3 15s from carol singing and sent it to Mrs Churchill with the wish that it should be spent on a lifebelt.

Women's Institute members were asked to bring a pinch of tea and their own sugar to the monthly meetings. Many of the men were active in the Home Guard. There was an anti-aircraft searchlight site in Benson Lane, close to the present village hall. (The wooden huts belonging to the searchlight were used by squatters for quite a long time after the war because there were not enough houses.)

One Crowmarsh man whose personal war history is particularly well documented is Will Wilder. When he came home in 1945, after three and a half years as a war prisoner of the Japanese, Will brought with him a and over 70 drawings of his experiences which he had hidden from his captors [11].

There is an obelisk in Wallingford at the junction of Wilding and Andrew Roads, commemorating the bravery and sacrifice of the flying officer and sergeant of a Canadian Halifax bomber, which on 9 September 1944 caught fire and crashed with a full bomb load on the Crowmarsh side of the River, east of Watery Lane. Five crew baled out, but by staying with their plane the two men who were killed saved a crash on Wallingford town. They had set out from Linton on Ouse to bomb L'Havre but were returning to base because of thick cloud over the target [12]. Exploratory digs in the summers of 1984 and 1985 revealed some of the remains of the plane embedded in the field. Earlier, in June 1940, three airmen from Benson were killed when their Fairey Battle crashed at North Stoke crossroads, just missing houses there.

As in any rural community, accidents happened on the farms, particularly when machinery was being used. John Blackall, for instance, was killed by a threshing machine at Mongewell in 1817 [13], and Joseph Wigley, a farm labourer of Crowmarsh Gifford, managed to walk home but died from injuries to his forearm after being drawn into a chaff cutter in 1894. An eight-year old Crowmarsh boy named Alfred Wheeler was kicked in the head by a horse when he was trying to pull its tail and he soon died of lockjaw; this was in 1884, long before anti-tetanus vaccines were available.

There were other occupational hazards. In 1901, George Dearlove, the Crowmarsh baker, slipped while taking a customer's dinner out of the oven and badly scalded his face and hands with hot grease. A 12-year old girl named Emily Brooks died after a serious dinner-time accident at Mongewell school in 1882. Screaming children alerted the schoolmistress, who found the girl enveloped in flames; she sustained such terrible burns that she died later the same day [14]. Also at Mongewell school, in 1905, during a science lesson a test tube being used in making oxygen burst, and little Lizzie Digweed got several pieces of glass in her face. A local doctor was usually summoned to these kinds of accidents, and the injured were sometimes conveyed to the cottage hospital in Wallingford.

Serious accidents occurred on country roads even before the 20th century. In 1868, nine-year old Edward Passey of Wallingford was run over and killed by a cart in Benson Lane as he was walking home from Benson school [15], and in 1890 a little boy named Summers was run down by a timber waggon near Mongewell Lodge, sustaining a bad head wound. Local newspapers generally reported such accidents. The arrival of the motor car brought more hazards. In 1913 there was a serious collision between two cars at the junction of Crowmarsh Street and Lane End. It took the assistance of about a dozen men to separate the cars involved; fortunately no-one was killed on that occasion. In 1944, a tanker collision at the corner of Benson Lane led to a fire that killed several American service men. Since the 1960s, several fatal car accidents have occurred in Crowmarsh, particularly along the formerly busy road past Howbery Park, a so-called 'black spot'.

Fires on the farms were not infrequent, sometimes with serious losses. In 1869, five and a half acres of barley belonging to Alfred de Mornay were lost; it was found that reapers smoking pipes were responsible. At Henry Allnatt's smithy in 1891 a cartshed and stable with much of their contents and a hayrick were destroyed. The cause of this fire was unknown, but for the unfortunate blacksmith it was his fourth fire in ten months. One Saturday in the 1930s a stack of straw bales caught fire in a field off Old Reading Road, where the school stands today. A colourful character named Freddie Luker was there, and in true Saturday form was the worse for drink. He wasn't going to let Mr Wilder's bales burn, so he got amongst them and threw aside all that he could, at

Thatch on fire at Newnham Croft, 1909.

considerable risk to himself. When the fire brigade arrived Freddie was in the way; the only solution was to play the hose on him, which it duly did.

The livelihood of Edward Hutton, a maltster of Crowmarsh Gifford who had premises in the Street, was threatened by at least two bad fires there. On 16 July 1756 a fifth of a ton of malt was lost [16], but worse was to come. On 14 February 1761 more than a ton was destroyed, although Edward was able to recover the excise duty that he had paid [17]. This was about the time of the disastrous fire at Howbery House (page 56).

Fire fighting arrangements were often quite inadequate before modern times, but men did their best. At the beginning of the 19th century Shute Barrington kept a fire engine at Mongewell Park, which was tested regularly. He duly noted in his when it was played, and the fact that it was in good order [18]. When a serious fire broke out at Coldharbour in 1983 firemen from Wallingford, Didcot and Goring attended, but still could not prevent the destruction of 4,000 bales of straw in the dutch barn.

We have many records of how the weather has played its part in the life of Crowmarsh folk. In years when poor harvests resulted from bad weather, people went hungry, and poor rates had to be raised. Large landowners alike were not spared the worry about their crops. At Mongewell, Shute Barrington voiced his concern in his diary. For instance, following a very high flood of the Thames, he wrote on 5 October 1774: 'Finished barley harvest, perhaps the latest ever known. A geat deal of it much damaged or entirely spoilt'. On 21 June 1795 it is recorded that severe cold had killed newly shorn sheep. An entry for 13 April 1775 reads: 'Sowed 1½ acres of carrots in Mill Close. Obliged to plough it up from dryness of the season'; and on 7 June 1787: 'Hard frost early - potatoes turned black'. By contrast the December 1773 carrot over a yard long and weighing three pounds would have provoked more favourable comments [19].

# War and Misfortune

Bad weather brought with it damage and destruction of all kinds. In particular, flood water from the Thames was a constant menace. The very high flood of 27 January 1809 brought water 16 inches deep into Mongewell church, and the next day Shute Barrington found six inches of water in his study and parlour at Mongewell House [20]. This was the occasion when the three principal arches of Wallingford bridge were so seriously damaged by flood water that it was necessary to rebuild them. Just downstream from the bridge, the greater part of the weir at Chalmore Hole Lock was carried away by the breaking up of ice after the great frost of January 1881 [21].

One of the worst floods was in November 1894, after it had rained almost daily for three weeks. The Thames overflowed so that by 15 November water extended from the church gate at Crowmarsh to a little beyond the Town Arms in Wallingford. Water rushed through five houses in the Street and it was deep enough to float a punt there. Henry Bowden's timber yard, opposite Bridge Villa, was under water for days

Thames flood in Crowmarsh Street, 1894.

and much damage was done to plant and stock. At Chalmore the large ferry boat broke away. Another repercussion of this flooding was that wells became filled with sediment and the Rural District Council had to request Alfred de Mornay and Charles Hedges, as local landlords, to clean them out [22].

In more modern times, the great flood of mid March 1947, after a thaw of heavy snow on frozen ground, took the river to about eight feet above normal.

In stormy weather trees at Howbery Park and Mongewell Park seem to have been very susceptible to damage, particularly the elms. A typical entry in Shute Barrington's reads: '31 December 1778. Very violent storm began about 11 pm and lasted all night. Some large trees were blown down'. One disastrous gale occurred on 21 March 1947 when, in less than an hour, nineteen trees fell on the stretch of road past Howbery Park, one killing a man riding a bicycle. In another fierce gale, four days earlier, four trees in the playground of Mongewell school were uprooted and three others were leaning so dangerously that they had to be felled.

Heavy snowfalls disrupted travel. In January 1814 drifts at Mongewell were said to be eight to ten feet high. Either the mail didn't get through at all, or eventually it arrived across the fields by evening [23]. During a great snowstorm in January 1881, local mails almost completely stopped; drifts were up to twelve feet high in exposed places [24]. In very snowy weather the children couldn't always get to school. On 20 January 1941, snowdrifts and bad roads meant that only nine out of 50 children arrived at Crowmarsh Gifford school; the next day seven came. During the severe weather of February and March 1947 the numbers of children attending were again very low.

Even in the coldest of winters the mill pond at Mongewell, emerging from a strong spring at a temperature of 10°C, was never known to freeze over, unlike the Thames. So it was from the Thames that ice was taken to fill the icehouse which was built in 1783 to supply Mongewell House [25]. The ice was loaded each winter any time between December and March when there was enough to cut; it usually took between 20 and 30 cartloads. The icehouse itself, a beehive-shaped brick structure, was unfortunately demolished in 1974 when the Reading Road was re-aligned at Icehouse Hill, despite last-minute attempts to save it.

# References

These are to printed and manuscript sources and are grouped by chapter. Books and maps are referred to by author; periodicals (including newspapers, journals and rolls series) are referred to by abbreviations, followed by date or by volume and page numbers. Manuscripts are referred to by abbreviations for sources (mostly record offices and libraries), followed by call mark.

**Books**

Medieval records published by:
a. Record Commissioners

    Nonarum Inquisitiones
    Rotuli Hundredorum
    Rotuli Litterarum Clausarum
    Taxatio Ecclesiastica P. Nicholai
    Valor Ecclesiasticus

b. HMSO

    Black Prince's Register
    Book of Fees
    Feudal Aids

# References

Allison, K J, Beresford, M W & Hurst, J G  1965  The deserted villages of Oxfordshire.
Allnatt, W  1873  Rambles in the neighbourhood of Wallingford.
Anderson, J R L  1974  The upper Thames.
Arnold, T (ed.)  1879  The history of the English: by Henry, Archdeacon of Huntingdon.
Baker, J H  1937  Land of the gap.
Baker, T  1869  History of the College of St John the Evangelist, Cambridge.
Bird, W H  1932  Old Oxfordshire churches.
Burke, J  1866  Extinct peerages.
Cokayne, G E  1887  The complete peerage.
Cole, B  1705  county map
Davis, R  1797  county map
Dewey, J & Dewey, S (eds.)  1983  Men of iron.
Dewey, J & Dewey, S  1985  POW sketchbook.
Ecton, T  1742  Thesaurus rerum ecclesiasticarum.
Emery, F  1974  The Oxfordshire landscape.
Gelling, M  1953  The place-names of Oxfordshire.
Gelling, M  1979  The early charters of the Thames valley.
Hartley, H  1939  Eighty-eight not out.
Hedges, J K  1881  The history of Wallingford.
Hedges, J K  1893  A short history of Wallingford.
Hobsbawm, E J & Rude, G  1969  Captain Swing.
Jennett, S  1976  The Ridgeway Path.
Jessup, M  1975  A history of Oxfordshire.
Kitchen, T  1753  county map
Lever, T  1947  The house of Pitt.
Lloyd, A  1966  The year of the conqueror.
McClatchey, D  1960  Oxfordshire clergy 1777-1869.
Martin, A F & Steel, R W  1954  The Oxford region: a scientific and historical survey.
Mee, A  1965  Oxfordshire.
Morden, R  1701  county map
Morris, J  1978  Domesday Book 14: Oxfordshire.
Potter, K R  1955  Gesta Stephani (The deeds of Stephen).
Philip, I G 1947, 1952  Journal of Sir Samuel Luke.
Relton, H E 1843  Sketches of churches.

Rodwell, K  1975  Historic towns in Oxfordshire - a survey of the new county.
Rowley, T  1978  Villages in the landscape.
Sherwood, J & Pevsner, N  1974  The buildings of England: Oxfordshire.
Skelton, J  1823  The principal antiquities of Oxfordshire.
Small, H G  1978  In and around Ipsden.
Stubbs, W (ed.)  1879  The historical works of Gervase of Canterbury, vol. I: The chronicle of the reigns of Stephen, Henry II and Richard I.
Taunt, H W  1878  A new map of the river Thames.
Thacker, F S  1968  The Thames highway (new ed.).
Tibbutt, H G  1963  The letter books of Sir Samuel Luke.
Warner, P  1968  Sieges of the middle ages.
Whitelock, D  1966  The Norman conquest.
Winbolt, S E  1932  The Chilterns and the Thames valley.
Wise, T  1979  1066 - the year of destiny.
Young, A  1813  General view of the agriculture of Oxfordshire.

**Newspapers**

| | |
|---|---|
| AH | Abingdon Herald |
| ARH | Abingdon and Reading Herald |
| BOA | Berks and Oxon Advertiser |
| JOJ | Jackson's Oxford Journal |
| OG | Oxford Gazette |
| OM | Oxford Mail |
| OT | Oxford Times |
| RM | Reading Mercury |
| WH | Wallingford Herald |
| WM | Wallingford Magazine |

# References

## Journals

| | |
|---|---|
| CA | Catalogue of Ancient Deeds |
| CC | Crowmarsh Chronicle |
| CChR | Calendar of Charter Rolls |
| CClR | Calendar of Close Rolls |
| CCRR | Calendar of Curia Regis Rolls |
| CFR | Calendar of Fine Rolls |
| CIPM | Calendar of Inquisitions Post Mortem |
| CN | Crowmarsh News |
| CPR | Calendar of Patent Rolls |
| CS 3 | Camden Society, 3rd Series |
| CS 4 | Camden Society, 4th Series |
| DNB | Dictionary of National Biography |
| GM | Gentlemen's Magazine |
| LPFD | Letters and papers, foreign and domestic, Henry VIII |
| LRS | Lincolnshire Record Society |
| NSIPM | North Stoke and Ipsden Parish Magazine |
| OAHS | Oxfordshire Archaeological and Historical Society |
| OHS | Oxford Historical Society |
| ORS | Oxford Record Society |
| OX | Oxoniensia |
| PGA | Public General Acts |
| PP | Parliamentary Papers |
| RASE | Royal Agricultural Society of England |
| VCH | Victoria County Histories |

## Manuscript Sources

| | |
|---|---|
| BdL | Bodleian Library |
| BrL | British Library |
| BRO | Berkshire Record Office |
| CGPC | Crowmarsh Gifford Parish Council - Minute Book |
| D | Deeds (with name of last known possessor) |
| HLRO | House of Lords Record Office |
| HRO | Hampshire Record Office |

# References

| NS | National Society |
|---|---|
| OA | Oxfordshire Archives (QS Quarter Sessions) |
| OCL | Oxford City Library |
| PRO | Public Record Office |
| REF | Royal Exchange Fire Insurance |
| RSL | Royal Society Library |
| SGL | Society of Genealogists Library |
| SIC | Sun Insurance Company |
| SMRO | Sites and Monuments Record Office, Oxfordshire County Museum |
| StJCC | St John's College Cambridge |
| StJCO | St John's College Oxford |

## 1 Settlements

**1** CGPC  **2** Gelling 1953  **3** Anderson 1974  **4** SMRO 8081, 12910  **5** Jessup 1975  **6** SMRO 2489, 7696  **7** OX 24:1-12; SMRO 3310  **8** OX 40: 122-135; Jennett 1976; ref 5  **9** SMRO 7692-7695, 7697  **10** Burke 1866, Cokayne 1887  **11** CIPM  **12** PRO C 132/31/1  **13** PRO C 133/47/13  **14** Feudal Aids  **15** LPFD  **16** HRO 43M4/117-8  **17** Morris 1978  **18** ORS 13: 1; Book of Fees  **19** BRO W/RT 6/138-9  **20** CClR 1248?9; Rot. Hund.; ORS 12: 222; CIPM 1286/7, 1360, 1372  **21** PRO PROB 11/115 (1610 will of Sir Wm Spencer); OA Misc Str III/i; BrL Egerton Ch 5741, Egerton MS 3567, Add MS 28672 f 291  **22** D, Messrs Walter Wilder & Sons  **23** ORS 15; Gelling 1979  **24** OA CJ/V/74, Misc Torr IV/12  **25** OHS 88: 271  **26** Rowley 1978  **27** SMRO 2194  **28** ORS 19  **29** PRO C 134/30/4 m 3; ORS 12: 67, 233  **30** PRO C 134/102/6/16  **31** CPR  **32** OHS 88: 234, 242, 268  **33** CChR  **34** CFR for 1437  **35** ref 31; PRO C2 JasII C15/61/3  **36** OA MS Oxf Archd Pp b41 f 57  **37** BRO D/Est L2  **38** BRO D/EH T81  **39** Ecton 1742; BRO D/P 161B 5/1; OA MS Oxf Dioc Pp d569 f 15, Davis 1797, Kitchen 1753, Cole 1705, Morden 1701  **40** CClR for 1368; Feudal Aids (1285); Blk Pr Reg 4, 412; CChR for 1281  **41** GM for 1826, 519  **42** OA MS Oxf Dioc Pp cl174, Misc Maples I/ii/9  **43** CCRR for 1208; Feudal Aids  **44** Feudal Aids; CChR for 1290; CIPM for 1311  **45** StJCO XXV.6; BdL MS Ch Oxon 233  **46** OA Misc Kent V/1  **47** BRO D/P 161/25/11  **48** RASE Ser III 1:57  **49** NSIPM Jan 1920  **50** Benson par reg 1761-1826; OA Cal QS rolls I: 255, VIII: 219, Davis 1797  **51** Skelton 1823  **52** CS 4 31: 382-389  **53** CGPC 20 Apr 1914  **54** CRDC 6; CGPC 17 June 1920  **55** CGPC 7 Aug 1942

## 2 The Land

**1** BRO W/RT 6/140  **2** BRO D/EH T67; OA 1668 will of John Clack  **3** PRO LR2/197, 224  **4** CGPC 18 Aug 1914; OA Crowmarsh I/2 Mar 1914  **5** CS 4 31: 382; BRO D/EH T81  **6** CIPM  **7** OA FC XI/1  **8** RSL MA 283

# References

## 3 Farmers

**1** OA QS   **2** OA QS   **3** OA Misc Torr IV/12; BrL Add MSS 28672 f 291   **4** PRO E179/162/260   **5** VCH Berks 4: 28   **6** ORS 21: 1-18   **7** BrL Egerton Ch 5741-5747   **8** OA CJ/V/74   **9** D, J Edwards, Coldharbour   **10** D, Walter Wilder & Son   **11** BRO D/EH T81   **12** OA CH/E/I/iii/4   **13** BRO D/P 161/8/1   **14** OA MS Oxf Archd Pp b40 f 107   **15** PRO E179/164/483   **16** BRO D/EH T67   **17** PRO C6/25/10   **18** OA Misc Tott IV/14   **19** OA QSD L92-95   **20** From F J Langford   **21** OA Misc Bucks VII/1   **22** ref 9; OCL CROWb 333.3   **23** DNB   **24** BRO D/Est L2   **25** CPR   **26** LPFD   **27** ref 24; PRO LR2/197, 224   **28** PRO C134/102/6/16   **29** PRO C2 Jas I C15/61   **30** OA MS Oxf Archd Pp b41 f 42   **31** From J Edwards, Coldharbour   **32** OA Misc St II/1   **33** OA Oxon c85   **34** SIC policy 180058   **35** Sale notice   **36** Young 1813   **37** OA MS DD Par Mongewell b1, c1; ORO QSD L93   **38** OA Misc Maples I/ii/9   **39** ORO Acc 918-I/i/6   **40** ORO PL XVIII/35; StJCC D86.14   **41** SGL Ac 6288   **42** Hartley 1936   **43** NSIPM   **44** D, B Park, Brook House   **45** 1928 sale notice; OA Misc Maples I/ii/9   **46** StJCO XXV 4, 5   **47** StJCO XXV 11, Reg III-Vi, IX, Gen Ledger 1730-59 p 232, Lease Bk 1760-78 p 99, Lease Reg 1778-84 p 90   **48** StJCO Reg II p 614   **49** StJCO Gen Ledger 1890-1915 pp 74, 285   **50** StJCC D86.1; CPR   **51** VCH Berks 2:80   **52** StJCC D86.29   **53** Baker 1869 p 450   **54** StJCC D86.3, 4   **55** StJCC D86.21   **56** StJCC D31.70   **57** OA QSD L95, 1812 will Francis King   **58** OA MS Oxf Archd Pp b41 f 58; StJCC D54.40, D86.20   **59** StJCO XXV.5   **60** OA Morrell II/i/4f   **61** OA Morrell ii/i/13a   **62** OA Misc Berks XXV/1   **63** OA SC 176

## 4 Houses

**1** Sherwood & Pevsner 1974   **2** RM 18 Dec 1965   **3** D, Carmel Coll.   **4** OA FC X/3   **5** Allnatt 1873   **6** OA Misc Maples I/ii/9   **7** RSL MS 262-313   **8** GM 1836 pp 297-302; DNB; OA MS DD Par Mongewell d1   **9** OA MS DD Par Mongewell c1   **10** PP 1830 XII p 153   **11** D, J Edwards, Coldharbour; JOJ 14 Jun 1833   **12** JOJ 24 Jul 1858; Allnatt 1873   **13** Hedges 1893   **14** BOA 24 Oct 1902   **15** CGPC   **16** Lever 1947   **17** OA MS Oxf Dioc Pp d561 f 177   **18** BRO D/EH T81   **19** OA Misc STII/1   **20** StJCO D of 1895   **21** OA Misc Maples I/ii/5   **22** NSIPM Nov 1929   **23** D of 1783, Morland & Co; OA QSD L92   **24** D of 1789, Morland & Co; OA QSD L92   **25** OA CH/E/I/iii/4   **26** D of 1791, Morland & Co   **27** Ds of 1767, Mrs B Pegge, Chaise House   **28** Ds, P G Summers, Days Cottage

## 5 Roads

**1** Emery 1974; Gelling 1953   **2** Martin & Steel 1954   **3** Anderson 1974; Rodwell 1975   **4** CC1R   **5** HLRO Public General Acts 5 Geo III cap55   **6** OA Misc St II/1   **7** OA Cooper Son & Caldicott 516   **8** ORO Acc 918/1   **9** CGPC   **10** CS 4, 31 p 382   **11** ORS 13, 14; OHS 88   **12** StJCC D 31.70, D54.40, D86.14, D86.20   **13** OA QS   **14** BRO W/RT 6/44   **15** ORO Misc Str II/1   **16** OA Newnham Murren Tithe Award   **17** 1796: RSL MA 286; 1808: OA MS Oxf Dioc Pp c2202 f 50   **18** OHS 88; CAD 3 p 526   **19** OA PL XVIII/35   **20** OA Crowmarsh I/9; D, J Edwards, Coldharbour   **21** BRO D/EH T67   **22** PRO PROB 11/405 ff 162-164   **23** BRO D/EH T68   **24** D, Morland & Co   **25** OM 11 Jul 1964   **26** OM 23 Mar 1967

## 6 The church

1 PRO E179/164/483; OA MS Oxf Dioc Pp d708; OA MS QS Cal IX p 716   2 OA MS Oxf Dioc Pp d556 f 121; d572 f 104; d573 ff 11, 13, 23   3 OA MS Oxf Dioc Pp c644 f 100   4 OA MS Oxf Dioc Pp d179 f 132   5 ORS 13 p 1   6 CPR 5 Aug 1391   7 VCH Berks 2 p 80   8 Val Eccl 2 pp 205, 207   9 StJCC D86.3   10 StJCC D86.21   11 StJCC D94.337   12 StJCC D86.62   13 Ipsden PR vol 2 fly leaf   14 OA MS Oxf Archd Pp b41 f 42   15 OA MS Oxf Archd Pp c327 f 30   16 OA MS Oxf Dioc Pp c449 f 11   17 OA MS Oxf Dioc Pp c661 f 35, b35 f 13   18 McClatchey   19 ORS 1 38, 97   20 OA MS Top Oxon d282 f 172   21 OA MS Oxf Dioc Pp c454 f 183   22 OA MS Oxf Archd Pp c141 f 25   23 OA MS Oxf Dioc Pp d555 f 157   24 OA MS Oxf Dioc Pp b41 f 76   25 OA MS Oxf Archd Pp b40 f 107   26 OA MS DD Par Mongewell d1   27 OA MS Oxf Archd Pp b41 f 57, 58; MS Oxf Dioc Pp c2202 f 50   28 Baker 1937   29 CS 3 73 127; OAHS 3 112   30 Hedges 1881 1 235   31 Relton 1843; BrL Add MSS 36372 f 227   32 Sherwood & Pevsner 1974   33 Bird 1932; OT 25 Aug 1882   34 BRO W/TH d2, d5; OA Misc Torr IV; CPR 1557   35 Tax Eccl P Nich 30   36 SMRO 2007   37 OM 9 Apr 1975; WH 22 Jan 1976   38 OA MS Oxf Dioc Pp c434 f 111v   39 OA MS Oxf Dioc Pp c1147; MS DD Par Mongewell D3; AH 30 Apr 1881   40 Winbolt 1932; Bird 1932; RM 12 Jun 1954   41 Sherwood & Pevsner 1974; Bird 1932   42 LRS 35 68   43 StJCC D 54.40   44 Bird 1932; Mee 1965; N Stoke Vestry Min Bk   45 NSIPM July 1925   46 OA MS DD Par Mongewell D3   47 D, D Strange   48 OM 4 Jun 1965; CC Feb 1967; PP 1837 XXVIII 304-306

## 7 Schools

1 OA MS Oxf Dioc Pp e22 f 62   2 OA MS Oxf Dioc Pp d558 f 176   3 OA MS Oxf Dioc Pp b40, c433, d566, 568, 570, 572, 707; PP 1819 IX p 722, 1835 XLII p 745   4 D(1850), Morland & Co   5 NS files   6 BdL Per 26221 e36   7 OA MS Oxf Dioc Pp c322 f 151; censuses and trade dirs   8 Crowmarsh Sch Man Min Bk, Mrs E Hasthorpe   9 From F J Langford, former pupil   10 OM 17 Nov 1956, 3 Aug 1959, 2 Feb 1962, 8 June 1962   11 OM 26 Nov 1971, 13 Jul 1973   12 OA Misc St II/1, MS Oxf Dioc Pp d179 f 277; censuses   13 OA MS Oxf Dioc Pp c433   14 OA OX.CRO T/SL 91   15 CC Aug 1971; OM 18 Oct 1974   16 NSIPM Sep 1935; StJCC Conclusions Bks; date stone   17 PP 1894 LXV

## 8 Craftsmen and Shopkeepers

1 PRO C 132/31/1, C 133/47/13   2 StJCC D 86.63   3 D, Morland & Co   4 OA FC X/1   5 OA Cal QS 1 185   6 OT 25 Aug 1882   7 REF policy 64147   8 BRO D/EH T68   9 BOA 29 Sep 1899   10 Dewey & Dewey 1983   11 OA MS Oxf Dioc Pp d556 f 121   12 BRO D/EH T81; OA Misc St II (D of 1857)   13 D, Walter Wilder (Ironfounders) Ltd   14 Warner 1968   15 Rot Lit Claus p 175; CFR (1228)   16 VCH Berks 3 534; CC1R (1268)   17 Non Inqu p 136

## 9 Services

1 Blk Pr Reg 4 126   2 Thacker 1968 vol 2   3 CGPC   4 OA Acc 918 I/5; OM 29 Sep 1956   5 CGPM; OM 25 Sep 1967   6 OA Acc 918 I/1; Crowmarsh I/3; CGPC   7 OA Acc 918 I/4   8 Small 1978

## 10 Sick and Poor

1 Hedges 1881 2 371   2 CS 4, 31 382   3 Hedges 1881 2 74, 371
4 VCH Oxon 2 155   5 BRO W/TH d4   6 CS 4, 33 166   7 CC1R   8 CPR
9 CPR; BRO D/EH T66   10 OA Misc Str III/1   11 Allison,
Beresford & Hurst 1965   12 Hedges 1881 2 384   13 Hedges 1881
2 177   14 OA Acc 918 I/1   15 OA Acc 918 I/4   16 NSIPM May 1913
17 Young 1813   18 OA MS DD Par Mongewell c1   19 OA Cal QS IV
419   20 NSIPM Jun 1920   21 PP 1830 XII 153   22 PP 1823 VIII 515
23 BRO D/P 161/25/11   24 PP 1823 VIII 526   25 NSIPM Feb 1935
26 OA MS Oxf Dioc Pp d708 f 160   27 OA Crowmarsh I/2, Nov 1895;
CN Dec 1986   28   E A Reade MS (G D Trentham)   29 PRO
C 6/436/56, C 10/281/54,57,58, C 10/283/26,63   30 PP 1823 VIII
515; OA Crowmarsh I/2, Nov 1895; CC Nov 1968   31 CN Mar 1981

## 11 Recreation

1 CPR 1340   2 BrL Egerton Ch 5741 (of 1651)   3 AH 9 Aug 1869,
3 Aug 1870; BOA 9 Aug 1895, 4 Aug 1899; OG 31 Jul 1954   4 OA
OX.CRO T/SL 91   5 CGPC for 1897, 1902, 1911   6 NSIPM Jun, Jul
1911   7 NSIPM Aug 1919   8 AH 9 Aug 1869   9 BOA 21 July 1899
10 CC Aug 1967   11 NSIPM Dec 1917   12 CC Apr 1972; CN Nov
1986; Crowmarsh WI Min Bk   13 RM 10 Nov 1962, 13 Nov 1965; CC
Jan 1968   14 OM 30 Nov 1954; CC Jul 1976   15 CN Oct 1981; D,
D Strange   16 OA Cal QS I 294; ORS 16 7   17 D, J Edwards,
Coldharbour   18 D, Mrs B Pegge, Chaise House   19 D, Messrs
Ushers   20 D, Morland & Co   21 OM 5 Oct 1967

## 12 Law and Order

1 CAPR 1323   2 Hedges 1881 1 360   3 JOJ 14 Sep 1771, 29 Feb
1772, 7 Mar 1772   4 JOJ 9 May 1789, 22 Jul 1789   5 JOJ 26 Feb
1763, 5 Mar 1763, 16 Jul 1763   6 JOJ 8 Jan 1831; Hobsbawm &
Rude 1969   7 JOJ 9 Mar 1776   8 OA QS/1700 Ea/34   9 N Stoke
Vestry Min Bk   10 PRO STAC 2 33/57   11 StJCC D 86.63   12 PRO
STAC 2 17/303   13 JOJ 19 Jan 1771   14 CGPC Apr 1895   15 NSIPM
Sep 1935

## 13 War and Misfortune

1 Whitelock 1966; Lloyd 1966; Wise 1979   2 Potter 1955; Arnold
1879; Stubbs 1879   3 Hedges 1881 1 235   4 Philip 1947, p 73
5 Philip 1952, p 255   6 Tibbutt 1963   7 Hedges 1881 2 141
8 StJCC SB 6.1 p 21   9 Crowmarsh Sch Log Bk   10 ORO T/SL 91
11 Dewey & Dewey 1985   12 CN May 1987   13 OA Cal QS IX 315
14 ORO OX.CRO T/SL 91; ARH 4 Nov 1882   15 AH 7 Dec 1868   16 OA
Cal QS III 509   17 OA QS Min Bk   18 RSL MA 298, 299   19 RSL MA
263-265, 277, 285   20 OA MS DD Mongewell d1; RSL MA 299
21 Taunt 1878; WM Apr 1981   22 BOA 16 Nov 1894; OA Acc 918
I/1/i   23 RSL MA 304   24 JOJ 22 Jan 1881   25 RSL MA 273

# Subject Index

| | |
|---|---|
| Abingdon | 60 |
| Accidents | 138 139 |
| Acres | 23 24 |
| Aircraft crashes | 137 |
| Alley, The | 90 |
| Allotments | 25 78 111 121 136 |
| Anabaptists | 65 |
| Arthur's Orchard | 37 |
| Assault | 27 30 129 |
| Bacon Lane | 63 |
| Bakehouse | 20 95 101 |
| Bakers | 17 95 138 |
| Bampton | 12 56 |
| Baptists | 65 |
| Barbican Close | 32 133 |
| Barges | 100 |
| Barrington | |
|     charity | 110 |
|     cottages | 43 44 109 |
|     diary | 26 43 140 142 |
| Basildon | 122 |
| Battle Abbey | 9 |
| Beaker folk | 6 7 |
| Bec Abbey | 72 |
| Beerhouses | 59 124 |
| Beersellers | 17 |
| Bell, The | 62 64 90 93 97 99 111 117 122 |
| Bennett's Barn | 46 |
| Benson | 23 61 70 88 126 |
|     airfield | 64 |
|     Lane | 21 33 54 64 77 79 94 118 124 137-139 |

| | |
|---|---|
| Bigg charity | 110 |
| Billy's Field | 121 |
| Blacksmiths | 17 64 90 |
| Black Death | 10 20 106 |
| Black Prince | 10 116 |
| Blenheim | 5 41 62 63 119 |
| Book of Fees | 11 |
| Botany | 25 |
| Boundaries | 7 12 20 23 102 104 |
| Brass memorials | 31 40 135 |
| Bridge Villa | 63 104 111 121 |
| British Legion | 84 |
| Brixton Hill | 12 62 |
| Bromhall Priory | 47 66 88 129 |
| Bronze Age | 6 7 |
| Brook House | 45 46 |
| Brooms Lane | 64 |
| Brownch | 41 |
| Bucklebury | 124 |
| Burchs Orchard | 32 |
| Burghfield | 45 |
| Burial places | 12 13 |
| Buses | 99 |
| Butchers | 97 100 102 |
| Candlemaker | 97 |
| Carmel College | 12 39 50 74 |
| Carpenters | 17 54 59 85 93 |
| Carrier | 99 |
| Catholicism | 65 |
| Catta's island | 13 |
| Caversham | 63 |
| Celebrations | 78 |

# Subject Index

Celts 7
Censuses 15 17 18 24 35 39 47 54 57
Chaise House 58
Chalmore Hole 100 141 142
Charities 25 58 109
Chatham, earl of 56
Chilterns 9 22
Chiltern Villa 64
Churches - see individual parishes
Churchwardens 41 49 77 93 107 110 112 113
Church Way 61-63
Civil wars 16 72 133
Clack's Lane 37 62 64
Clack's Orchard 32
Close Rolls 10 11
Clubs 119 120 122
Coach and Horses, The 124
Coach builder 92
Coldharbour 18 33 38 84 140
Col d'Arbres - see Coldharbour
Commonwealth Agricultural Bureaux 51
Common fields 23 24 46
Common land 24
Constables 27 29 30 36 41 59 127 130 131
Cook Lane 6
Coronations 103 117
Cottages 20 43
Cottars 10
Cottingham charity 110
Council houses 21
Cox's Lane 21 25 64
Craftsmen 88
Creswell's Farm 41

Cricket 57 119
Crops 22
Crop marks 6
Crowbrook 23
Crowmarsh
  by-pass 24 64 85 121
  civil parish 5 72 78
  crofts 23
  fair 116
  Farm 21 34
  fetes 118
  field 23 111
  forts 132
  hill 12 64 94 106
  hospital - see Leper hospital
  market 10 97
  name 5 10 20
  Street 12 23 30 60 62 87 90-92 95 100 102-104 115 124 138 141
Crowmarsh Area Social Benevolent Society 120 125
Crowmarsh Battle 10 127
Crowmarsh Chronicle 125
Crowmarsh Gifford
  church 31 72 73 75 115 126 133 135
  malthouse 89
  manor house 31 33
  Parish Council 25 103 121 136
  rectory 70
  school 79 83 102 119 120 136 142
  tithe barn 35 71
  village hall 85 115 119 121 135
  village pump 101

## Subject Index

| | |
|---|---|
| Crowmarsh News | 125 |
| Crowmarsh Parish Council | 121 |
| Crowmarsh Rural District Council | 135 |
| Curates | 66 70 |
| Dairy House | 33 |
| Dame schools | 85 |
| Day's Cottage | 59 97 |
| Diphtheria | 84 106 |
| Dodd charity | 110 |
| Domesday Book | 9 11 20 88 |
| Dorchester | 61 |
| Dormer Cottages | 21 |
| Dorrell charity | 110 |
| Dorrell's Farm | 45 46 59 |
| Drains | 102 |
| Drincan | 63 |
| Drunken Bottom | 63 |
| Durham, bishop of - see Barrington | |
| Electricity | 49 102 |
| Emery charity | 25 111 113 |
| Employment | 17 18 |
| Empress Matilda | 72 104 132 |
| Enclosures | 23 |
| English Farm | 109 |
| Evacuees | 84 86 136 |
| Ewelme | 11 13 63 |
| Ewelme Way | 63 |
| Exciseman | 90 |
| Eyots | 13 25 |
| Eyre Rolls | 126 |
| Farmers | 17 27 |
| Farrier | 90 |
| Fernleigh | 37 |
| Ferry | 100 142 |
| Feudal Aids | 10 |
| Feudal system | 8 |
| Fine Rolls | 10 13 |

| | |
|---|---|
| Fires | 56 139 140 |
| Fire insurance | 41 90 |
| Fisheries | 9 26 40 |
| Fisherman's Green | 26 |
| Floods | 19 22 140 |
| Football | 119 122 |
| Footpaths | 77 135 |
| Forest Row | 20 43 63 |
| French Gardens | 21 55 |
| Friendly Neighbours | 120 |
| Gales | 142 |
| Gambling | 130 |
| Gamecock, The | 21 25 94 124 |
| Gamekeepers | 11 94 |
| Gangsdown Hill | 62 |
| Gardeners | 17-19 124 |
| Gardeners Arms, The | 92 94 102 124 |
| Gas supply | 102 |
| Giffords Concert Party | 115 |
| Giffords, The | 58 120 |
| Glebe | 24 35 48 69 71 |
| Glovers | 36 |
| Goldes | 47 |
| Golf course | 120 |
| Goring | 60 77 |
| Goring Priory | 66 |
| Grange, The | 49 |
| Gravel pits | 62 |
| Grocers | 91 96 99 |
| Grim's Ditch | 8 12 13 62 |
| Hackney Way | 63 |
| Hagbourne | 95 97 |
| Hagioscope | 74 |
| Hailey | 45 |
| Hailey Way | 25 61 64 |
| Hampstead Norreys | 114 |
| Harvest Home | 38 |
| Harwell | 49 |

# Subject Index

| | | | |
|---|---|---|---|
| Hearth tax | 16 31 36 40 41 48 52 | King Charles I | 133 |
| Hedges | 23 62 | Edgar | 12 |
| Henley | 61 134 | Edward I | 105 |
| Henley Way | 12 25 60 61 | Edward III | 11 |
| Hitchin | 23 24 111 | Edward VII | 120 |
| Home Guard | 137 | George V | 39 103 117 |
| Home Farm | 37 39 41 92 | Henry II | 11 97 98 132 |
| Howbery | | Henry III | 10 98 105 |
| Farm | 27 30 33 38 90 92 106 | Henry VIII | 11 13 47 70 105 128 |
| gas works | 102 | James II | 67 |
| House | 38 39 55 | John | 98 |
| military camp | 55 | Richard II | 66 |
| name | 11 | Stephen | 11 72 98 132 |
| Park | 18 54 64 79 118 142 | William I | 9 132 |
| Place | 56 | Kings Court Rolls | 11 |
| refugee camp | 55 | King's evil | 67 |
| Hydraulics Research Ltd | 54 | Knight service | 8 |
| Hydraulics Research Station | 56 | Labourers | 17 |
| Icehouse | 143 | Lamplighter | 103 |
| Icehouse Hill | 8 62 63 143 | Land tax | 32 37 38 95 |
| Ickleton Way | 63 | Land use | 9 22 |
| Icknield Way | 8 9 12 60 61-63 | Lane End | 21 37 62 71 138 |
| Iffley | 115 | Lay subsidies | 36 41 |
| Ilsley, East | 31 | Leper hospital | 20 61 74 104 |
| Institute of Hydrology | 56 | Limeburners | 94 |
| Inventories (probate) | 22 23 25 34 35 42 45 46 48 52 67-69 71 89 114 | Limes, The | 57 95 |
| | | Lincoln, bishop of | 48 76 |
| | | Littlemore | 115 |
| Ipsden | 15 32 45 47 49 59 63 67 68 86 112 | Little Stoke | 31 |
| | | Livestock | 23 |
| Iron Age | 8 | Llandaff, bishop of – see Barrington | |
| Iron foundry | 32 90 131 | Lonesome | 5 41 |
| Isolation hospital | 106 | Long Crowmarsh | 20 |
| Jubilees | 117 | Lot Mead | 22 |
| Kilmorey, earl of | 12 56 | Malthouses | 32 89 |
| Kimberley Cottage | 46 47 120 | | |

## Subject Index

| | |
|---|---|
| Maltsters | 89 |
| Manors | 8 24 |
|   Benson | 9 104 |
|   Crowmarsh | 10 20 |
|   Crowmarsh Gifford | 10 24 |
|   Howbery | 11 24 33 56 65 106 |
|   Newnham | 12 13 |
|   Newnham Murren | 13 |
|   North Stoke | 14 15 46 |
|   Stoke Basset | 14 |
| Marsh Lane | 24 62 63 |
| Marsh, The | 24 |
| Mass dial | 76 77 |
| Meadows | 22 |
| Meadow Lane | 90 |
| Measles | 84 |
| Medieval times | 8 9 23 67 |
| Middle Farm | 47 |
| Milking Path | 24 |
| Millers | 88 89 |
| Mills | 7 19 88 |
| Mill Close | 71 |
| Mill ponds | 26 51 57 71 142 |
| Mongewell | |
|   church | 50 52 54 74 141 |
|   Farm | 43 |
|   fire engine | 140 |
|   gas works | 102 |
|   hospital | 50 |
|   House | 51 52 68 89 92 141 |
|   manor house | 14 89 |
|   mill | 89 126 |
|   monument | 54 |
|   name | 5 |
|   Park | 50 118 140 142 |
|   Park Farm | 43 |
|   rectory | 68 69 102 107 |
|   schools | 53 85 102 110 117 138 142 |
|   shop | 53 109 110 |
|   tithe barn | 71 |
| Moulsford | 49 |
| Muddy Lane | 62 63 |
| Murder | 117 126 |
| National Society | 79 80 |
| Nettlebed | 126 |
| Newnham | |
|   crofts | 20 21 23 102 |
|   Farm | 14 25 39 56 114 |
|   field | 23 105 |
|   House | 57 103 118 |
|   name | 5 13 14 |
|   Wood | 41 |
| Newnham Murren | |
|   church | 20 74 75 |
|   manor house | 12 14 39 56 |
|   school | 85 |
| Newnham Warren | 14 |
| New Town | 20 |
| Normans | 9 20 |
| North Stoke | |
|   church | 46 76 128 135 |
|   dental clinic | 107 |
|   Farm | 49 69 86 |
|   manor house | 46 |
|   mill | 43 57 88 |
|   parish room | 120 |
|   post office | 97 |
|   school | 49 86 120 |
|   shop | 59 97 |
|   street | 49 |
|   tithe barn | 71 |
|   vicarage | 48 67 68 |
|   village green | 78 |
|   village hall | 21 86 118 120 |
| Nuffield | 8 36 61 99 |
| Orchards | 31 32 37 40 |
| Owen charity | 58 111 |
| Oxford, bishop of | 68 84 |
| Oxford, earl of | 11 |
| Oxford Way | 64 |
| Parish Councils | 78 |

# Subject Index

Parish House 78 85
Parish magazines 124
Parish Meetings 78 84
Parish registers 15 18 40
Park View 21
Pembroke, earl of 10
Photographer 17 78 97
Pigeonhouses 31 32 48
Pipemakers 17 94
Plague 105 106
Plymouth Brethren 41
Pocock's Farm 49
Poor rates 107 108 140
Poors cottage 111 123
Population
  mobility 18
  size 10 15
Port Way 25 63
Post Office 93 95-97 100 128
Presbyterians 65
Prince Charles 51
Prospect House 59
Publicans 17
Quarry 94
Quarter Sessions 11 59 61 94 108 127
Queen
  Elizabeth I 13 40
  Elizabeth II 118
  Victoria 117
Queens Head, The 36 123
Radcliffe Infirmary 69
Reading Abbey 13 20 63 104
Reading Road or Way 56 62 63
Recreation grounds 121 122
Rectors
  Crowmarsh Gifford 58 61 65 70
  Mongewell 13 66 68
  North Stoke 48 67

Rectory Farm 24 30 47 48 71 88 108 135
Redundant Churches Fund 74
Retreat Cottages 21
Rewley Abbey 126
Ridgeway Farm 45
Rod Eyot 25
Romans 8
Roselea 58
Rough Music 128
Royal Air Force 50
St John's College, Cambridge 47 66 86 129
St John's College, Oxford 47 57 79
Sanctuary 126
Saxons 8 13 20 23 63 66 72
Scarlet fever 107
School
  dinners 84 137
  log books 80 81 137
  milk 84
  swimming lessons 84
Schools 57 79 80
  see also individual parishes
Shalbourne 29
Shearman's Lane 64
Sheepcot 13 43
Shepherds 17 18 86 128
Shepherds Lane 64
Shoemakers 17 59 80 93
Shopkeepers 17 94 95
Skeletons 7 13
Smithy 90 91
Smith charity 111
Snowstorms 142
Soils 22
South Oxfordshire District Council 55

# Subject Index

| | |
|---|---|
| South Stoke | 106 |
| Springs | 6 13 19 62 88 |
| Springs, The | 15 49 57 |
| Stadhampton | 97 |
| Stagecoaches | 99 |
| Star Chamber, Court of | 128 |
| Steers Lane | 64 111 112 |
| Stockbridge | 23 111 |
| Stockbridge Lane | 64 |
| Stocks | 127 |
| Stoke | |
|   name | 5 |
| Stoke Row | 72 99 109 |
| Stone Age | 5 |
| Street lighting | 30 78 102 |
| Strips | 23 |
| Suffolk, duke of | 11 |
| Suffolk, earl of | 13 |
| Suicide | 130 |
| Sundials | 46 |
| Sweating sickness | 105 |
| Swing riots | 127 |
| Swyncombe Way | 62 |
| Tailors | 17 94 108 |
| Tallowchandler | 97 |
| Teachers | 80–82 93 |
| Telephone | 101 |
| Tennis | 119 |
| Terriers | 23 24 35 45 48 69 71 |
| Thames | 5–9 12 22 26 100 132 140–142 |
| Thatchers | 94 |
| Theft | 27 29 127 |
| Three Cocks, The | 123 |
| Threshing machines | 91 138 |
| Threshing mill | 43 |
| Tidgeon Way | 60–63 104 |
| Timber yard | 94 |
| Tithe | 71 |
|   barns | 35 71 |
|   maps | 24 32 35 56 |
| Traffic lights | 64 |
| Transportation | 127 |
| Tudor times | 23 62 |
| Turnpikes | 61 |
| Unemployed | 94 |
| Uphill Farm | 41 |
| Upper Farm | 45 |
| Upper House Farm | 43 45 |
| Vet | 90 |
| Vicars | |
|   Crowmarsh Gifford | 66 |
|   North Stoke | 48 67 |
| Village | |
|   sites | 19 |
|   sizes | 20 |
| Wallingford | |
|   bridge | 13 60 61–64 88 100–102 106 107 126 132 134 141 |
|   Bridge Estate Charity | 115 |
|   castle | 13 48 132 134 135 |
|   cottage hospital | 54 |
|   school | 31 |
|   workhouse | 108 130 |
| Wall paintings | 76 |
| Warden or Warren Hill | 12 |
| Water supply | 78 101 107 |
| Watery Lane | 12 62 104 119 126 137 |
| Watlington Way | 64 |
| Wells | 101 142 |
| Wheelwrights | 17 29 91 92 |
| White Hill | 128 |
| White House, The | 124 |
| Wicks | 58 |
| Wittenham, Lord | 55 |
| Wix Way | 46 61 64 |
| Women's Institutes | 120 137 |
| Woodcote | 101 |
| Woodhouse Farm | 8 45 |
| World War I | 21 50 135 |
| World War II | 57 84 86 136 |
| Yardland | 35 47 |

# Name Index

| | | | | |
|---|---|---|---|---|
| Absolon | 43 124 | | Bristow | 49 61 69 |
| Alden | 112 | | Brooks | 138 |
| Alderman | 37 | | Brown | 58 120 |
| Allibone | 29 33 | | Burden | 81 107 |
| Allnatt | 32 33 37 46 47 58 89 90 95 127 139 | | Burgess | 32 79 |
| | | | Butler | 34 36 |
| Allen | 50 | | Butt | 59 77 118 120 |
| Anderson | 135 | | Cailly | 116 |
| Andrews | 99 | | Caine | 49 |
| Arthur | 34 36 42 | | Cardinal | 67 |
| Arundel | 47 | | Cass | 67 |
| Astley | 68 | | Chapman | 82 |
| Bacon | 63 | | Chaucer | 13 |
| Barnard | 40 135 | | Chester | 30 |
| Barrett | 29 130 | | Cheyney | 35 |
| Barrington | 14 17 26 43 44 51 53 69 71 74 85 109 110 124 140 141 142 | | Clack | 34 35 36 65 89 109 |
| | | | Clare | 65 92 93 |
| | | | Clark | 90 |
| Bartholomew | 35 | | Clarke | 38 43 88 89 |
| Basset | 14 | | Cliff | 40 |
| Belcher | 80 93 | | Collier | 92 |
| Bennett | 46 59 | | Comber | 65 |
| Bereford | 13 | | Cook | 43 |
| Bigg | 31 32 36 110 122 | | Coombes | 124 |
| Blackall | 112 123 138 | | Cooper | 45 |
| Blackstone | 12 18 32 54 72 79 122 | | Cope | 11 30 |
| | | | Copelin | 96 |
| Blisset | 32 | | Corderoy | 88 |
| Bolbec | 11 66 | | Cottingham | 32 33 110 122 |
| Bolter | 88 129 | | Cottrell | 45 |
| Bowden | 92 141 | | Cox | 64 90 |
| Bradford | 58 | | Crane | 27 |
| Bradshaw | 67 129 | | Creswell | 41 58 97 |
| Brant | 94 124 | | Crispin | 13 |
| Briggs | 49 | | Crook | 101 |

# Name Index

| | |
|---|---|
| Croughton | 131 |
| Cros, du | 55 |
| Crump | 48 |
| Cummins | 32 |
| Dale | 125 |
| Dams | 124 |
| Danby | 58 |
| Dandridge | 97 100 102 |
| Dawson | 93 |
| Day | 40 59 114 |
| Dean | 13 39 |
| Dearlove | 95 96 97 138 |
| Debren | 94 96 |
| Deely | 93 |
| Digweed | 138 |
| Dodd | 45 46 49 86 110 |
| Dore | 84 |
| Dormer | 48 135 |
| Dorrell | 46 71 88 110 |
| Dunsden | 91 |
| Durell | 69 70 |
| Dust | 81 |
| Dyer | 90 |
| Edwards | 37 39 43 136 |
| Ellen | 97 |
| Emery | 27 36 40 68 111 113 115 116 |
| Exlade | 126 |
| Field | 115 |
| Fortescue | 13 40 |
| Foster | 36 93 |
| Fraser | 14 45 50 69 86 89 118 |
| Freeman | 85 |
| Fry | 127 |
| Fuller | 40 |
| Gibbons | 134 |
| Giffard | 9 11 |
| Goff | 86 |
| Goodall | 127 |
| Goshawk | 97 |
| Gough | 93 |
| Gould | 14 50 92 |
| Grant | 124 |
| Gregory | 106 |
| Guilding | 89 |
| Guise | 14 52 |
| Gul | 107 |
| Guttridge | 78 97 |
| Harbert | 48 |
| Harcourt-Smith | 39 |
| Harrison | 127 |
| Hartley | 46 |
| Hasthorpe | 85 136 |
| Hastings | 10 |
| Hatchman | 128 |
| Headlam | 68 |
| Hedges | 12 14 57 142 |
| Herbert | 43 |
| Hicks | 127 |
| Higgs | 37 42 59 97 106 |
| Hildesley | 30 65 106 |
| Hill | 59 |
| Hodson | 68 |
| Holmes | 122 |
| Honey | 96 |
| Huberd | 105 |
| Hughes | 69 |
| Hurst | 123 |
| Hutton | 89 140 |
| Jacobs | 97 |
| Jewsons | 89 94 |
| Johns | 58 |
| Keats | 30 32 33 |
| Keen | 49 |
| Kennerley-Rumford | 59 77 |
| King | 19 48 70 85 93 96 108 |

# Name Index

| | | | |
|---|---|---|---|
| Kitchen | 33 37 96 | Painter | 45 |
| Knight | 58 | Palmer | 97 122 |
| Langford | 37 | Parker | 32 67 |
| Lay | 93 96 | Parsons | 38 |
| Lea | 70 | Passey | 138 |
| Lee | 18 122 | Paul | 14 |
| Lewenden | 96 | Pauling | 39 |
| Loader | 31 | Payton | 94 |
| Lock | 97 | Peachie | 67 |
| Longland | 67 | Phillips | 94 |
| Loveday | 14 126 | Pitt | 56 |
| Lovegrove | 92 124 | Plested | 136 |
| Luke | 134 | Price | 14 43 51 69 71 |
| Luker | 91 139 | Rathbone | 82 |
| Manley | 40 | Read | 32 |
| Marks | 112 | Reeves | 59 |
| Marshall | 10 | Restwold | 11 |
| Mercer | 39 | Reynolds | 80 |
| Merrison | 124 | Roberds | 42 |
| Moeles | 15 | Roberts | 70 88 95 97 |
| Molins | 14 48 52 | Rowden | 43 |
| Moores | 35 37 | Sadler | 34 35 36 71 |
| Morin | 13 63 104 | Sarney | 123 |
| Morland | 122 124 | Saunders | 14 52 69 94 |
| Mornay, de | 18 37 39 54 77 118 139 142 | Selwood | 58 69 70 |
| | | Skinner | 39 105 |
| Morrell | 49 120 | Slater | 46 |
| Morrison | 122 | Smith | 33 41 65 91 93 94 96 108 111 |
| Moss | 94 96 | | |
| Nailer | 124 | Spyer | 123 |
| Nedham | 12 24 33 37 38 56 79 | Stamp | 43 60 |
| | | Stapleton | 14 |
| Newman | 127 | Stephen | 57 122 |
| Norris | 93 | Stonor | 14 30 47 |
| North | 65 | Summers | 138 |
| Owen | 58 111 | | |

# Name Index

| | |
|---|---|
| Thomas | 68 |
| Titler | 82 83 |
| Toovey | 14 40 41 43 56 57 96 |
| Trentham | 49 |
| Trollope | 65 70 79 |
| Trulock | 70 |
| Tucker | 35 99 |
| Tull | 27 28 31 33 |
| Turner | 95 |
| Twopeny | 86 |
| Usher | 123 |
| Valence | 10 |
| Vaux | 74 |
| Vere | 11 |
| Wadley | 127 |
| Wakefield | 54 |
| Walsh | 57 103 |
| Warcopp | 109 |
| Watkin-Williams-Wynn | 54 |
| Watters | 99 123 |
| Wells | 123 |
| Westall | 29 |
| Wheeler | 138 |
| Whichelo | 47 |
| White | 107 |
| Wickens | 102 130 |
| Wicks | 58 86 127 |
| Wigley | 138 |
| Wilder | 58 59 90 131 137 139 |
| Wilkins | 31 |
| Williams | 45 |
| Willis | 27 |
| Willsden | 58 |
| Wilmot | 29 |